Local Nurseries for Local Communities

The history of neighbourhoods and their future prospects

By Doreen McCalla, Chris Grover and Helen Penn

NATIONAL
CHILDREN'S
BUREAU

making a difference

The National Children's Bureau promotes the interests and well-being of all children and young people across every aspect of their lives. NCB advocates the participation of children and young people in all matters affecting them. NCB challenges disadvantage in childhood.

NCB achieves its mission by
- ensuring the views of children and young people are listened to and taken into account at all times
- playing an active role in policy development and advocacy
- undertaking high quality research and work from an evidence based perspective
- promoting multidisciplinary, cross-agency partnerships
- identifying, developing and promoting good practice
- disseminating information to professionals, policy makers, parents and children and young people

NCB has adopted and works within the UN Convention on the Rights of the Child.

Several Councils and Fora are based at NCB and contribute significantly to the breadth of its influence. It also works in partnership with Children in Scotland and Children in Wales and other voluntary organisations concerned for children and their families.

The views expressed in this book are those of the authors and not necessarily those of the National Children's Bureau.

Published by National Children's Bureau Enterprises Ltd, the trading company for the National Children's Bureau, Registered Charity number 258825. 8 Wakley Street, London EC1V 7QE. Tel: 020 7843 6000

© National Children's Bureau, 2001
Published 2001

ISBN 1 900990 71 7

British Library Cataloguing in Publication Data
A catalogue record for this book is available from the British Library

Typeset by Jeff Teader
Production by L.P.P.S., Wellingborough NN8 3PJ
Printed by Impress Print, Corby NN18 3EW

Contents

Acknowledgements   v

Abbreviations   vii

1 Setting the scene   1
2 Community nurseries in context   5
3 Community nurseries now   17
4 Case study one – Ackroyd Under Fives Nursery   35
5 Case study two – Robert Owen Early Years Centre: Continuity and
   change   41
6 Case study three – Marcus Garvey Nursery: Catering for the black
   community   47
7 The end or just the beginning? Community nurseries in neighbourhoods   65

Appendix 1 – The nurseries in the survey   79
Appendix 2 – Experiences from the chalk face: Stories from parents
   and workers   81
Notes   89
Index   105

Acknowledgements

The production of this book has been both enjoyable and rewarding, although extremely challenging. It could not have been completed without the help of many people working in various settings across the country.

Special thanks must go to Syble Morgan, the first Head of Marcus Garvey Nursery, for her tireless efforts in the study of Marcus Garvey specifically and community nurseries generally.[1] We are also grateful to Jean Leader, Head of Ackroyd Under Fives and Judy Stephenson, Head of the Robert Owen Early Years Centre, for devoting their time to a presentation of their nurseries at a national community nurseries workshop which was held in November 2000. Many of the presentations were developed into the chapters in this book. Thanks also to Sue Downing, Caroline Patrick, Marcia Myers and a parent from Foundation Nursery for sharing their personal stories, which are also included in this book.

We are most grateful to members of the Community Nursery Collaborative Working Group[2] who offered useful advice, information and documentation concerning local and national community nurseries, and participated in the recent community nursery workshop. In addition to the people mentioned above, the group also includes Eulalee Brown and Lorraine Williams of SADWCA; Betty Davies of HACH Nursery; Naseem Khalifa of Whitmore Reans Community Day Nursery; Suzanne Lowe of Lyncroft House; Rose Robinson of Bacchus Road Nursery; Pat Rocester of Marcus Garvey Nursery; Mary State of Foundations Day Nursery; Nicky Stubbs of St Paul's Nursery; Lorraine Tullock of Bournbrook Community Day Nursery; Annmarie Hassell and Sandra Jenkinson of Birmingham EYDCP; Caroline Field and Joe Roach of Nottingham EYDCP; Debbie Harris, Sharon Hindley and Lynn Lynock of Wolverhampton EYDCP; Collette Kelleher of DfES; Jenny Brown of Quality Childcare Support Services; Sarah Tooze of Sheffield Community Childcare Network; Kenneth Dunkwu of BUILD-Nottingham; Samuel Edgar and Julia Johnson of the Salvation Army and Morwenna Griffiths of Nottingham Trent University.

In addition, we very much appreciate the help of the many staff of community nurseries and EYDCPs who allowed us access to their work settings, and generously gave their time to participate in lengthy interviews and to complete our questionnaires. We are also indebted to those parents whose children attend or used to attend community nurseries and those people involved in community nurseries who also gave of their time to talk to our researchers.[3] Furthermore, we thank Samuel Edgar and Julia Johnson of the Salvation Army, who provided their Citadel (church) as the venue for the community nurseries workshop and, along with Hazel Seabridge, helped in accommodation planning for the event.

In supporting us in the various research projects upon which this book is based, we thank the following people: Pauline Graham, Lucy Lloyd, David Noble and Jennifer Ryder of the Daycare Trust; David Noble (childcare consultant) for helping with interviews and mailings; Charlie Owen of the Thomas Coram Research Unit and John Stewart of Lancaster University for their help and advice on issues concerning questionnaire design and data analysis; Annie Woods of Nottingham Trent University for the initial information literature; Cheryl Scott and Jean McCalla for transcribing taped interviews; N Raynes and H McLaughlin for their undertaking of research on EYDCPs for the Children's Society; and also to Emma Moore, Bethany Rawles and referees of the National Children's Bureau, and Pat Farrington, freelance editor, for publication advice and support.

Finally, for funding the projects on which this book is based, we thank the Department of Health, Bridge House Estates, the Children's Society, AW.60 Charitable Trust and Nottingham Trent University.

Abbreviations

CCP	Certificate in Childminding Practice
DfEE*	Department for Education and Employment
DfES	Department for Education and Skills
DHSS**	Department of Health and Social Security
ESF	European Social Fund
EYDCP	Early Years Development and Childcare Partnership
GCSE	General Certificate in Secondary Education
GLC***	Greater London Council
HACH	Holyhead Association of Community Help
IT	Information Technology
NCS	National Childcare Strategy
NVQ	National Vocational Qualification
OECD	Organisation for Economic Cooperation and Development
Ofsted	Office of Standards in Education
SADWCA	Sandwell and District West Indian Community Association
SRB	Single Regeneration Budget

*   the DfEE is now the Department for Education and Skills
**   the DHSS is now two separate departments – the Department of Health and Department of Social Security
*** the GLC is now abolished and unitary councils operate instead

1 Setting the scene

This book came about because of two main reasons.

First, it emerged from a workshop on community nursery provision that was held in Birmingham in November 2000. This workshop brought together individuals who had some knowledge of community nurseries in the context of childcare and early years policies and practice, and was attended by 39 people from community nurseries, Early Years Development and Childcare Partnerships (EYDCPs), local authorities, religious and voluntary sector groups and universities. In addition to attending formal presentations, participants could engage with the work of some community nurseries that had stalls at the workshop. These stalls demonstrated the ethos, aims and activities of the nurseries. This book is based upon papers and presentations at the workshop. It brings together academic research on community nurseries and their position within the wider context of early years policies, practice and welfare reform, and the thoughts of workers who run community nurseries and parents whose children have attended them.

The second reason relates to policy. In 2000, the Government announced its intention to develop a Neighbourhood Nursery Initiative to increase the number of childcare places (not necessarily new nurseries) available to parents living in disadvantaged or socially excluded communities. This idea raised important questions about how such communities are already serviced by daycare provision. Was the Neighbourhood Nursery Initiative starting from scratch? Or was there existing provision that could be learned from? This book demonstrates that there are indeed such provisions that policy makers and administrators might examine to develop a more coherent approach to meeting not only the developmental needs of children, but also the needs of their parents and the communities in which they live.

The book aims to discuss the context in which community nurseries were established, how they are currently running and their potential role under the new Neighbourhood Nursery Initiative. As we show, there is confusion over what a community nursery is.

This is evident in much of the existing literature on childcare which often makes little distinction between community and private nurseries [1,2,3] or acknowledges the differences but then goes on to combine the two [4,5,6]. This book attempts to unravel the confusion by looking at current research and presenting the experiences of those involved in running and using the services of community nurseries.

The structure of the book

The aims of the book are tackled as follows. Chapter 2 examines the context of community nurseries. It discusses the early years context by examining the position of community nurseries within the fragmented nature of early childhood provision that presently exists in England. The chapter then goes on to discuss the historical development of community nurseries from the early 1970s. It focuses on its original aims of the community nursery movement and the ways in which some of them are undermined by political and social change. It ends by examining some of the issues raised by the community nursery movement – some of which, 30 years later, are yet to be resolved.

Chapter 3 is concerned with more contemporary community nursery provision. It is based upon a survey of community nurseries in England that were identified by specific characteristics. The chapter examines their contribution to the high profile, New Labour policy aims of welfare reform and tackling social exclusion. We show that existing community nurseries have much to offer in these areas because, in addition to providing affordable childcare, they often provide services that help to increase the self-confidence of parents and therefore increase their chances to access education and/or paid employment. However, this chapter also shows that many community nurseries face a paradoxical situation. Although they are providing services that fit with government priorities, they also face funding constraints that threaten their services because of the market-led approach of the National Childcare Strategy.

Chapters 4 to 6 are case studies of community nurseries. Chapter 4 is about Ackroyd Under Fives Nursery in Lewisham, London, Chapter 5 focuses upon the Robert Owen Early Centre in Greenwich, London, and Chapter 6 examines Marcus Garvey Nursery in the Handsworth area of Birmingham. The case studies chart the histories of the nurseries, examine their operating ethos and the practicalities of running not-for-profit nurseries. What these case studies demonstrate is that while there is no single model of a community nursery, their aims and objectives are similar in attempting to meet the needs of children, their parents and the wider community by providing services that go beyond the provision of childcare.

Chapter 7 draws the book to a close by returning to discussions of community nurseries in the context of the fragmented and contradictory nature of early years services in England. It concludes that while community nurseries should not be supported for the sake of it, they do have an important role to play in New Labour's early education and childcare policies, and provide an opportunity for coordinating services for children and their parents.

Appendix 2 contains the stories of three people who are currently, or in the past have been, involved with community nurseries. These stories were told at the community nurseries workshop. They have been included to give a voice to parents of children who have attended community nurseries and the workers there. They also help verify, as do the case studies in Chapters 4 to 6, the findings of the wider studies of community nurseries discussed in Chapter 2.

2 Community nurseries in context

This chapter describes community (or neighbourhood) nurseries and looks at the traditions they draw on.

The fragmentation of nursery provision

In the UK there is considerable confusion about what nursery provision is for and who should deliver it. The plethora of names to describe the various kinds of services for young children, and the regularity with which the press and public confuse them, illustrates the problem. There are the new neighbourhood nurseries, which are not so much nurseries but places made available in any kind of nursery for children at risk of 'social exclusion', because of where they live. There are also nursery classes and nursery schools; early years units and reception classes in schools; community nurseries, playgroups and community playgroups; day nurseries; family centres; early years centres; centres of early excellence; private nurseries; crèches; childminders and nannies.

Functions as well as names have changed. Thirty years ago, nursery schools offered free full time education and daycare for children aged two to five or even six, although it was not a statutory service and not all local education authorities chose to provide it. Nowadays, nursery entitlement is defined as part time education (no more than morning and afternoon shifts of two-and-a-half hour sessions in school terms) for four-year-old children, who may stay as little as two terms. Parents who want more than the part-time nursery entitlement must seek (and pay for) wrap-around care, which provides childcare for the extra hours over and above the short nursery education hours. Often this wrap-around care is provided by different people in a different place and operating to different standards of nursery education. This is a confusing, and even disturbing, arrangement for very young children and also often poses problems for parents who have to make the arrangements. Yet because the Government has defined the nursery education entitlement as operating separately and for different purposes in the National Childcare Strategy, these administrative categories must be followed through at every level. Young children themselves do not usually experience continuity of care and education.[1] Our early education and care system, if nothing else, is therefore a tribute to the resilience of the children who use it!

Early years provision can be grouped very broadly into three types of provision:

■ Education provision which employs qualified teachers, has an explicitly educational remit. It operates on educational terms and conditions and is a free entitlement.

■ Care for vulnerable children or children in need, which employs care or social workers, has a protective remit. It focuses on family support and may be full time or, more commonly, part time.

■ Childcare or daycare for the children of working mothers, which is chosen and bought by mothers mostly from the private sector, includes childminding and private day nurseries. This sector has increased considerably over the last four years, much of the growth being in large, commercial/private day nursery chains.

Despite the central division between education, which is free at the point of use, and childcare, which must be paid for, the Government has attempted to blur the differences between the many kinds of early years provision. This has been done in a number of ways:

■ All forms of provision taking children aged three and over, from every sector, are now expected to deliver a standardised 'foundation stage' curriculum.

■ All forms of registered provision for any age child must submit to a centralised regulatory and inspection system administered by Ofsted. However, this inspection system is still different for nursery education delivered in maintained nursery schools or classes, where more rigorous educational standards are applied.

■ The funding allocation for the nursery education entitlement may be awarded to the maintained or the non-maintained sector at the discretion of the EYDCPs.

a) For forms of provision at least 50 per cent of staff must have Level 2 NVQ or above, with the exception of maintained nursery schools and classes, where teaching regulations apply, and qualified teachers are in charge of, and deliver, the nursery education.

Provision is mostly planned and delivered through EYDCPs, which are supposed to bring together all providers under the aegis of a lead officer from the local authority.

It is a complicated system. The recent Organisation fo Economic Cooperation and Development (OECD) report on early childhood education and care in the UK notes that although there have been considerable improvements:

> the administrative and conceptual divide between childcare and early education is felt keenly in the field where local authorities and partnerships struggle to meet the regulatory and funding requirements of the different initiatives.[2]

In England, there are many different kinds of provision, most of which operate somewhat rigidly in terms of the hours there are available, the charges they make and where they are sited. England has refused to opt for a system, as in most other European countries, where there is a standard form of local provision for every child, for example, the *écoles maternelle* in France, or kindergartens in Sweden, which operate as flexibly as possible and serve *every* local community. Parents in England, paradoxically, could be said to have *less choice* even though there is more diversity of provision. Put another way, in England, the choices people have depends on their income. The higher the income, the more options are available to a family, including transport to and from the service and nannies to bridge any gaps.

Communities and neighbourhoods

The Government is increasingly concerned about 'social exclusion', that is, the lack of opportunities available to poor families and/or poor neighbourhoods, and the alienation this can produce. At the time of writing, the latest proposal is for 'neighbourhood nurseries' to enable children from such neighbourhoods or families to benefit from childcare. However, as usual, these proposals are put forward without any specific reference to the system of nursery education. It is possible to develop a nursery school into a neighbourhood nursery, as one of our examples shows. But in this neighbourhood initiative, for the most part, the emphasis in the Government documentation has been on creating more places in already existing private and voluntary provision[3]. Instead, we believe that it is necessary to locate the role of community or neighbourhood nurseries in the light of a wider debate about community cohesion specifically, and the coherence and delivery of services generally.[4]

'Community' and 'social exclusion' are difficult concepts to explain. Many of the (ex)local authority housing estates on the edge of towns and cities represent – at least geographically – clearly defined poor communities. On the other hand, in inner London, where child poverty is greatest[5], and in some other cities and rural towns, wealth and poverty are typically cheek by jowl. For example, in a short London street where one of the authors lives, there are big owner-occupied houses, rented accommodation, council flats and squatters. In some houses people may have lived there for more than 40 years. In others, the turnover is so fast no one is recognisable. There are barristers, doctors, artists, musicians and salesmen, as well as mini-cab drivers, cleaners, receptionists, building workers and a few marginalised families. There are residents who came originally from Nigeria, Latin America, Cyprus, China and Serbia as well as those who were born in the UK. The street is multi-generational. There are a number of elderly retired white people, widows and widowers, a few new babies, and a few children (very few nowadays), who ride their bicycles and play outside. How does one describe this area or street as a community or work out who is socially excluded within it?

Maybe the Nigerians belong to a wider kin community; the Latin Americans and the Serbs possibly see themselves as part of a refugee diaspora. Most people belong to a number of loose and overlapping networks through work, family, religion, exile or personal interests. Permanence, continuity, solidarity and mutual interest may characterise some communities, but for fewer and fewer people this is now the case[6].

These ambiguities about what constitutes a 'community' are reflected in the case studies that we include in this book. One community nursery is based on a very local, self-defined geographical catchment in a mainly working class district of terraced houses; another is based on an education catchment, as defined by the local authority. A third nursery defines its catchment primarily in ethnic, rather than geographical, terms. It is a very difficult question whether or not such diverse interests can, or should, be included as part of policies that aim to provide equity of access for all children.

The community nursery movement

There have been various popular nursery movements in the UK. The earliest was probably that of Robert Owen at New Lanark in 1816. The community nursery movement described in this book began in the late 1970s and early 1980s. It developed mostly in inner city areas, partly growing out of urban aid programmes, although it received its biggest impetus in London from the Greater London Council (GLC). This body had a specific policy to support such initiatives and many nurseries set up in the 1970s and 1980s received their initial funding from the GLC. The importance of the community nursery movement is that it represents a determined and detailed attempt to engage in dialogue about the position of nurseries in their local communities and the roles they might fulfil. The movement has never been documented properly, so the examples do not represent a definitive overview.[7]

Community nurseries were attempts, often feminist-inspired attempts, to challenge the status quo. The received wisdom up till then was that it was wrong for mothers to work. Maybe working-class women or single parents had to work out of economic necessity, but, middle-class mothers were advised and expected to stay at home. The traditional rhetoric about respectable family life was very strong and had been given a new impetus by the attachment theories of John Bowlby in the late 1940s and early 1950s. He argued that a warm, strong, continuous bond with a mother figure (although this was often misinterpreted as a biological matter) was essential for healthy psychological development and without it children were at risk of becoming delinquents. It is now widely argued that mothers, particularly lone mothers, can do their children more good by demonstrating a role model connected to the formal economy[8] – clearly, an example of just how much ideas (and perceptions) change over time.[9]

The Plowden Report on Primary Education, published in 1967, announced very firmly that it was not the duty of the state to encourage mothers to work. It was at that point nursery education switched from being mostly full time to mostly part time. Playgroups, too, were very set against working mothers. In fact, 20 years ago their rhetoric was very offensive towards them, although this has now clearly changed. Council-run day nurseries offered some places to working single parents, whose children were automatically defined as being 'in need' but these council day nurseries usually had long waiting lists. Middle-class mothers who chose to work full time were regarded as being exceptional and a series of books tried to pinpoint what made them so unusual. Now the wheel has come full circle. Statistically speaking, it is middle-class mothers who work, and working-class mothers and single parents who stay at home.[10]

Many of the community nurseries grew out of a feminist, collectivist view of childrearing because of a sense of unease with the official view about mothering. One of the first community nurseries was based in London. It was called 123. It was set up in December 1972 in a short-life tenancy house in a mixed community in North London, opened from 8.30am–6pm and took a maximum of 15 children at any one time. It was staffed by one full time and one part time member of staff and a rota of volunteers, and was funded by a small annual grant from the local council. Its aims were:

- To have a very small local nursery so all families were within walking distance and children were in a home-size environment.
- To provide a meeting place for everyone in the immediate neighbourhood, from old age pensioners (OAPs) to teenagers at school.
- To be run collectively by parents and staff and not as part of a professional service or bureaucracy.
- To involve fathers and other men.
- To provide situations and activities that question what boys and girls have traditionally been expected to do.
- To give children the opportunity to question the status quo about what happens around them and to live and share with others.
- To provide services to empower local women.

There were a number of issues with which 123 continually struggled. One was about professionalism:

> We agree totally on the need for all staff to be paid, but some
> people in the collective question the need to exclude
> 'unqualified people' and are suspicious of what constitutes
> qualification in areas involving children. It is not that they deny
> that childcare requires skill, patience and experience – what they
> fear is the tendency of professional people to hide behind their
> status and cut themselves off from ordinary people.

Another, more obliquely expressed, issue concerned class and race. This manifested itself in arguments about who should volunteer and what could be expected of volunteers in running the nursery. Middle-class women were more used to activism. Working-class women did not view volunteering in the same way. They were less confident and did not have the same flexibility in the labour market, and if they were working, found it more difficult to combine it with volunteering their time:

> To some extent the centre has been an alien imposition on an
> already depressed area and in terms of people involved, most of
> whom were middle class women ... part of the point of 123 can
> be for people who have not had this kind of experience or
> background to gain that experience, to learn how to struggle
> collectively for what they want (and to learn that can be
> enjoyable as well) and to take back some of the power that has
> been alienated from them.

Other issues concerned the constant drain of having to apply for and juggle with funding. In fact, the 123 collective came to the conclusion that what would work best was not more community nurseries but much more flexible mainstream education provision that adopted many of the ideas of the community nursery movement but was properly resourced. One of the founder members of 123 went on to become a primary school head teacher.

However, as we have seen, the aim of traditional education provision was to reproduce traditional social relationships and maintain the status quo, while an essential aim of 123 was to try to challenge traditional social relationships:

> we do not want to reproduce the social relationships presented in society at large, and are trying to develop different ways for children to relate to each other and to adults. We want to work against the competition and individualism that capitalism encourages and thrives on, and to break down hierarchies and challenge authority figures ... we refuse to believe that competition, individualism and hierarchies and authorities are all part of human nature, and we believe it is possible to rear different kinds of people: people who can work together, who support and care for each other and who are sensitive to each other's needs. How do we do it? How can we begin to change things?[11]

123 articulated their problems very explicitly and often painfully. But they typified many of the community nurseries, which, in their annual reports and campaigning leaflets, made a case for the kinds of nurseries they wanted. Some of this material was collected by the forerunners to the Daycare Trust, the London Childcare Campaign and the National Childcare Campaign. Some of these nurseries were, for a short time in the early 1980s, supported by a DHSS grant to the National Childcare Campaign and evolved as part of the grant-giving process, but they foundered as the grants were subsequently withdrawn. The aims of the community nursery movement originally can be summarised as:

■ *Small is beautiful* – ideally a house in every street set aside for a nursery/community meeting place.
■ *Locally managed* – nurseries managed themselves and decided their own policies rather than being an arm of a statutory service.
■ *Collective* – no managerial-speak or professionalisation but an attempt to resolve day-to-day and long-term strategies through discussion and collective agreement with everyone involved.

- *Local workers* to staff the nurseries, drawn from the community that is being served.
- *Catchment based.* Catchment, rather than income, determines access. The nurseries were open to everyone within a certain radius.
- *Affordable.* Some nurseries operated a low flat-rate fee, others charged fees according to household income, but no one in the catchment was to be turned away through inability to pay. This meant that the nurseries were dependent on public grants and funding.
- *Intergenerational.* Young children are community members along with the staff, older children and adults of all ages who surround them, and they all have a common interest in the place where they are.
- *Equality.* Women must be supported as workers not just as mothers; similarly, men must be supported as fathers not just as workers.
- *Cohesive.* Care and education functions are properly integrated from the point of view of the child.
- *Children are not a different species.* Children have wit, imagination, originality and the capacity to care. They can best exercise these talents by taking part in everyday activities alongside others, rather than in an environment which exclusively concentrates on a narrow age range of children.

Then and now?

The socialist-feminist sentiments which shaped the community nursery movement seem to have vanished from consciousness. In the present market-driven climate, they might read as hopelessly naive and dated. 123 and many of the other nurseries disappeared, as short-life tenancies expired and GLC and council grants dried up. However, it is worth pointing out that at about the same time a similar group of nurseries, with very similar aims and a collective ethos, were set up in Reggio Emilia, northern Italy. They, and others like them, had consistent and systematic public support and went on to become world famous nurseries – a pilgrimage centre for early years specialists.[12] In fact, 123 and other such community nurseries were, without knowing it, in some cases, part of an international movement which led to collective nurseries being set up in Germany, France, Spain and Italy, where mostly they have survived and become an essential part of the early years landscape, such as the state-run *crèches parentales* in France; the collective nurseries in northern Italy and Spain; and the cooperatives in Germany.[13, 14] But in the UK there was no such development. Community nurseries struggled on in the margins of mainstream provision and was mainly dominated by the private sector.

A recent study indicated that there are now many nurseries that call themselves 'community nurseries'. However, the criteria by which they were included in the study were that they were usually self-managed, non-profit making, voluntary day nurseries.[15] The community nurseries listed include some of the original community nurseries, but their day-to-day survival mostly precludes any such ideological commitment. Non-profit making nurseries have been forced to take anyone who can pay the fees, although in their provision of subsidised places local children tend to take precedence. The local community orientation appears to have been diluted but not abandoned. A graphic account of the current difficult circumstances of one of these community nurseries was given recently to the House of Commons Select Committee on Education.[16] The fees charged to parents simply did not meet the staff bill and workers, some of them long serving, were forced to take cuts in salary or even to work voluntarily. Funding is obviously a critical issue. Even with tax credits and increased benefits for individual parents, in a competitive market increasingly dominated by nurseries owned by chains[17], community nurseries in poor areas find it hard to survive.

But the community nurseries movement has raised questions that have still not been addressed. Firstly, community nurseries were, to an extent, *anti-professional* and *anti-hierarchical*. Professionals were perceived to have narrow sectoral interests. But they were also seen to represent conventional ideologies at the time about mothering and, as the experience of the Marcus Garvey Nursery suggests, about race. Community nursery activists were less concerned about the rights or wrongs or strengths or weaknesses of one profession over another – health or education or social work – than by how professionals in general could be circumvented. Government discussions on delivery of services now contain many references to 'joined-up thinking'. The Sure Start programme, for example, aims to bring diverse professionals together in the interests of young children in the community. By contrast, the community nursery movement brought mothers and local activists together to challenge the views of professionals. The nurseries ran themselves despite the antagonism of professionals. Views towards mothering have changed, but there are still current examples of local women challenging professional wisdom about childcare and how children should be treated.[18]

Can local people get together – without professional intervention – to organise the local facilities they want? The hundreds of applications to the GLC for community nurseries from tenants' groups, small voluntary groups and others suggested that they could. At the Ackroyd Nursery, the voluntary secretary for several years was a single mother from an African-Caribbean background, who at the time was in a hostel for homeless families. She had been referred on to Ackroyd because the local social services department considered her to be very difficult to handle. However, many of the groups applying for funds did reflect the mixed social class of the kinds of neighbourhood described above. This social mix is likely to have shaped the kinds of debates taking place amongst the groups and given them the confidence to challenge established norms. Perhaps, in more monotypical settings, with more marginalised groups, and now with a much tighter childcare regulatory system, such activism may be harder to achieve.

A second key issue for the original community nursery movement was about the extent to which they could be seen as a model of social action for the wider community. Many of them operated alongside, or offered, other services to the community besides care and the education of young children. The three community nurseries described here all have additional functions – for example, the OAP club at Ackroyd, the support for the black community at Marcus Garvey, and the community cyber-cafe and drop-in facilities at Robert Owen. Similar roles were found in our survey of community nurseries: for example, a community remembrance garden at The Bridge Nursery and IT training at the High Peaks that could be accessed by young people from the local youth centre. Community nurseries saw themselves as being integral to their local community and its regeneration. The ambition of the original community nursery movement was also to change social relations in the nursery, and through this offer a model of collective organisation in which social solidarity was an important feature.

A third issue for the community nursery movement was to accord young children – and childhood itself – more dignity and more self-determination. This is neatly put by the coordinator of Ackroyd: 'we wish we could just let children be'. This perspective, that although children live in the here and now (as we all do), our nursery and school practices focus on shaping their lives in terms of what we want them to become, is now the subject of much academic and policy debate. Inspired by the UN Declaration on the Rights of the Child, many advocacy groups now have projects about 'listening to children'. There is an increasingly prominent view that children's views, even young children's views, on the services they use, should be actively sought.[19] In most countries, the statutory school starting age is six or even seven. In England most children have already begun primary school by the age of four. This practice is regarded as very odd outside the UK, because it expects too much of children too soon.[20] The community nursery movement regarded childhood as a time for self-directed exploration and very informal learning. At the same time, they insisted that young children should not be treated differently from anyone else. They should not be segregated from other age groups in specialised institutions, but should live inter-generational lives. Hence the importance of the 'community' side of community nurseries.

But the regulatory, as well as the funding, framework for early years has changed considerably. It is much harder to be innovative and original when standards are rigidly imposed from the outside, unless creativity is mustered from within the imposed standards. Compared with most other European countries, where some degree of self-regulation is usual, England has an externalised, centralised regulatory system, with relatively punitive outcomes for those who fail to meet the criteria.[21] Quality control is more tightly, if narrowly, defined and breaches of perceived quality mean loss of funding, as well as loss of status in a competitive market. The original community nurseries had the leeway to challenge received wisdom on a range of issues including gender, religion, race relations, children's self-determination and the values of social solidarity. This freedom to challenge the status quo is less likely to be the case under the new regulatory regimes.

Finally, a critical issue for the old community nurseries was accessibility. Many of them operated a clear catchment policy, and within their catchment area everyone, no matter what their background, was entitled to use the service on a first-come-first-served basis. This was possible because they were directly grant-aided. Our experiences suggest that indirect funding of services makes it more difficult to achieve community involvement and representation. At present, the National Childcare Strategy (although not education provision) has adopted a system of indirect funding of services that funds users through the 'tax credit' system, to enable them to 'choose' childcare in an open market. But the market cannot operate in poor areas because the profits are insufficient and the capital investment too risky. The OECD report[22] cited on page 7 is unequivocal that better quality and more *accessible* services are likely to emerge through direct funding rather than through a market system where parents buy childcare in a competitive market place.

In the end, the question arises, did the community nurseries in the 1970s and 1980s make a significant difference to the children and parents who used them? The evidence is anecdotal. This book has arisen because the authors were, respectively, involved with Ackroyd over a 21-year period, and Marcus Garvey's twenty-fifth anniversary. It seems that, though not statistically proven, the outcomes for the children who attended were indeed better than might have been expected from the intake. For instance, at a fifteenth anniversary party at Ackroyd, not only did all of the first cohort turn up, but they had all done well in their GCSEs and were taking A levels. The children who attended Marcus Garvey also seem to be doing better than predicted from comparable African-Caribbean groups. This would be an interesting topic for further research.

The community nursery movement raises interesting questions for current policy making. Can a community nursery contribute more to the community than regular childcare places? The history of community nurseries suggests that they can.

3   Community nurseries now

Introduction

This chapter is based upon the first national survey of community nurseries in England. It discusses the contribution that community nurseries make, particularly in the context of the current political focus upon welfare reform and the tackling of social exclusion. It examines differences between not-for-profit, community-based daycare, private and state sector nurseries.

Researching community nurseries[1]

We have seen in chapter 2 that, on the whole, community nurseries were set up because of the demands of parents (mostly mothers) in response to the chronic shortages of daycare places in particular localities. The nature of the community nursery movement, in particular the local character of individual campaigns, meant it was difficult to track community nurseries. In contrast to organisations such as the Pre-School Learning Alliance and the National Childminding Association for pre-school children, or registered childminders, community nurseries have no central organisation to represent their interests, and perhaps, in any case, do not form a coherent group.

Finding out the names and addresses of community nurseries so that questionnaires could be sent to them was the first obstacle we faced. To do this, the first phase of the research involved writing to all local authority registration and inspection units in England to see if they could provide us with information on community nurseries in their areas. This exercise raised a second major issue. How should we describe community nurseries to local authority staff so that they gave us information on the relevant nurseries? The idea was to use defining characteristics of community nurseries. However, as we have seen, the aims of the community nursery movement were many and varied, from the provision of small locally-based childcare to a rejection of hierarchy and professionalisation. Some of these characteristics were patently too impractical to use. Could we expect, for example, registration and inspection units to know if any of the daycare providers on their books were organised along collectivist lines? What if such principles no longer applied to a nursery although it remained outside the private sector?

In the end, in a covering letter, we sent a list of four characteristics that we thought could be easily used by registration and inspection units in the identification of community nurseries in their area. The characteristics were that:

- the children attending the nursery would be from the area immediately surrounding the nursery;
- there would be a commitment to be open five days a week for the whole of the day to allow parents to work full time;
- parents would be involved in the management of the nursery;
- the nurseries would be run on a not-for-profit basis and usually (but not always) have charitable status.

In practice, however, even this list of characteristics was too much for some registration and inspection units – they did not have the relevant information or did not have it in an accessible form. As it turned out, the most important defining characteristic was that the nursery was run on a not-for-profit basis. The characteristics relating to management committees and the areas from which children were drawn became less important for two reasons. First, it became clear – and with hindsight perhaps this is not surprising – that registration and inspection units often had little idea of where children lived in relation to the nurseries they attended and the nature of the management structures of the nurseries. Second, it was apparent that some community nurseries, while attracting children for subsidised places from specific areas (for example, postal code areas), had no restrictions on the areas from which they would take children in fee-paying places. The characteristic relating to opening hours was tightened so that only those opening for eight or more hours were included. So while we write about community nurseries in this chapter, the survey was actually of daycare provision:

- open for at least eight hours a day;
- run on a not-for-profit basis.

This was the best definition for a community nursery that we could manage. Through this phase of the research, 256 community nurseries were identified throughout England.

The second phase of the research involved sending a questionnaire to each of the nurseries identified. The questionnaire addressed issues relating to the children attending the nursery, staffing matters, costs and finances and the services offered by the nurseries beyond their central focus of providing all-daycare. The response rate to the survey was 48 per cent.

We then interviewed in depth the managers and some of the parents using nine community nurseries.[2] From managers the aim was to obtain a more detailed view of the issues facing the nursery and how they felt the nurseries related to the local community. Parents were asked to talk in detail about what they felt the nursery meant to them and their children and the wider community. The nine nurseries were chosen, first, because they agreed to partake in in-depth interviews (something that relatively few agreed to do) and, second, to ensure a geographical spread across England. Brief descriptions of the nine nurseries are contained in Appendix 1.

Social exclusion, welfare reform and the National Childcare Strategy

On being elected in 1997, New Labour argued that one of the most important issues by which its first term in Parliament could be measured was its ability to reform Britain's welfare system. After four years in office, substantial developments in what is defined as a process of modernisation of welfare have taken place. These developments include the various new deals for unemployed people and lone parents (read lone mothers), the Working Families' Tax Credit, the Childcare Tax Credit, the National Minimum Wage and the National Childcare Strategy. The aim of these developments is to change the nature of the British 'welfare' system, from a 'something-for-nothing welfare state'[3] to a 'something-for-something deal for those out of work that will change the culture of the welfare state'.[4] In other words, continuing arguments from the 18-year reign of the Conservatives, the existing welfare state was held to encourage a 'dependency culture', most particularly the rejection of paid employment in favour of a life wedded to state support through social benefits. To overcome this debilitating state of affairs, a new pro-active system was deemed to be necessary, a system 'to reward [paid] work, not irresponsibility'.[5]

The message from New Labour is clear: acting 'responsibly' means being in paid employment. Those who are not in paid work are acting irresponsibly and need to be 'encouraged' into work. The aim of New Labour's welfare reform package has therefore been to get those of working age who are able to do so into paid employment. All the major developments listed above are aimed at achieving that through the carrot of financial incentives and the stick of benefit withdrawal – the result of not taking advantage of existing job opportunities. In this line of thinking, welfare is to become a 'hand up not a hand out'.[6] The belief is that the 'best form of welfare is [paid] work'.[7]

The National Childcare Strategy is an important element in this process of welfare reform. The Prime minister, Tony Blair, has described it as 'the first plank of our [New Labour's] welfare reform programme'.[8] The strategy is crucial if the government is determined to reduce the number of people who are not in paid employment and receiving social security benefits instead. It is hoped that the National Childcare Strategy will break the 'childcare barrier' which is seen as the main factor against employment for lone mothers particularly.[9]

The question remains, why does New Labour place such importance on the relationship between paid employment and welfare reform? There are important economic reasons for increasing the closeness of the relationship between the receipt of benefit and paid employment.[10] There is also the aim of tackling social exclusion at a more individual level. In this sense, the promotion of paid employment is important because it is defined as 'the best anti-poverty, anti-crime and pro-family policy yet invented'.[11]

This focus upon tackling social exclusion through paid employment has important implications for the National Childcare Strategy. It is in the most excluded – the poorest – communities that there is a lack of childcare. As Sally Holterman has pointed out, in poor communities the market has failed.[12] The private sector does not earn sufficient profits and risks capital investment in poor areas. The introduction of the recent Neighbourhood Nursery Initiative, through which it is hoped that, by 2004, 45,000 new nursery places will be developed to serve deprived communities, is a recognition of this failure. The aim of neighbourhood nurseries is to ensure that 'there should be a childcare place in the most disadvantaged areas for every lone parent entering employment'. It addresses the needs of communities where 'thousands of lone parents and low income families still feel that their childcare commitments stop them from working'.[13]

Funds for building or developing existing premises are to be made available through the New Opportunities Fund, while funding over three years is to be made available to help with start-up costs to help establish the new nurseries. After that period, the nurseries will be left to meet their costs (and, in the case of private nurseries, make a profit) from fee revenue.

There is a contradiction that goes to the very heart of this policy, for it is those same disadvantaged communities in which the new neighbourhood nurseries are to be established that the private sector has been vacating for many years as they are unprofitable. There is a danger that any market-led solution of delivering childcare will merely exacerbate already existing divides between communities with relatively good and relatively poor access to high quality daycare. It is here that existing community nurseries have a useful role to play. The absence of a profit-making motive means that they do not face the commercial pressures of private nurseries and hence they are more able to operate in the most disadvantaged communities. So, for example, half (49.2 per cent) of the community nurseries identified in the survey of registration and inspection units were found to be in the 20 most deprived local authorities in England. Three-quarters (76.2 per cent) were located in the 100 most deprived local authorities in England.

Second, as we have seen, many community nurseries offer services that go beyond just the provision of childcare, to meet some of the wider social and economic needs of their communities, which neatly fit into the Government's concern with social exclusion and getting people into paid employment.

Tackling social exclusion at a community level

The idea of social exclusion has become closely associated with the integration of non-employed people into labour markets. Welfare policy is being re-aligned to reward financially those in low paid employment. This means that if non-employed people want to increase their incomes significantly in the future, they will have to take paid employment. Those who, for whatever reason, cannot take paid work will be left to flounder on inadequate out-of-work benefits such as income support. However, leaving aside the fact that in many areas there is still not enough work for all non-employed people to take, the process of finding employment can be a long haul. When seeking employment a person has to have confidence and the characteristics that employers desire. Those characteristics may include a particular level of education and/or specific skills. If non-employed people have been out of labour markets for many years, they may lack both confidence and relevant skills and qualifications.

Community nurseries are important in this respect because they often offer services that go beyond the provision of childcare. Over half (55.8 per cent) of respondents noted that their nursery was part of, or attached to, a larger project in the community. The services often aim to help build the confidence of parents and help them directly to access education, training and work. So, for example, the most frequently mentioned projects that those nurseries were part of, or attached to, were those helping parents to return to work through education or training. This was followed by projects such as the provision of drop-in sessions to reduce isolation in the local community, help people with English language skills, improve the health of local people and help them to return to work through job search advice or skills development.

Building confidence

> The media describe us [lone mothers] as being scroungers, lazy buggers who don't want to work and live off the state. This just isn't true, but it means I don't have very high self-esteem.[14]

In the recent past, governments have been successful in stigmatising lone mothers as being the cause of a host of social and economic problems, including delinquency, the misuse of illegal substances, unemployment among young men and underage sex. With the media as their allies, recent governments have attempted to create an atmosphere of what Ginsburg called 'social less eligibility' – a feeling of stigmatisation.[15] However, as the lone mother above notes, there is a contradiction with this process. It involves feelings of low self-worth and a lack of confidence that may prohibit the one thing – paid employment – that lone mothers can be 'encouraged' to do to demonstrate the right role models to their children.[16]

Before contemplating taking employment, many lone mothers will have to boost their self-esteem. Community nurseries can play an important role in this process. Linda, whose children attended High Peaks while she attended a *Build Your Skills* course there, said, for example:

> I'm a lot happier [since attending the course] ... You actually want to get up in the morning and get dressed, instead of dossing on the settee all day and being miserable ... And it's time to prove to yourself that, not for anybody else, but yourself, that you are capable of doing things. That you are capable of learning, that you are intelligent. Just 'cos you've got kids, you're not thick or 'owt. You are intelligent. You have got something to offer.

She connected her increasing confidence, and that of her peers, to educational achievements they were enjoying on the courses offered at High Peaks:

> Before we took the exams … we'd been given these mock papers
> and we thought 'oh God we can't do that. We're crap. We can't
> do nothing'. Now we've all got these results and I'm never saying
> that about myself again, ever.

The manager of High Peaks also highlighted the ways in which the nursery and
courses run in its training room were helping local women develop their confidence
to meet their potential:

> **Manager** Some of the ladies that we are training were finding it
> very daunting to actually approach colleges or to go university
> and to actually make that first step into further education, so
> High Peaks is really a sort of ideal setting for parents who want to
> gain the confidence and build up their return to work skills.
>
> **Interviewer** So it's about confidence as well as learning?
>
> **Manager** That's right. Confidence and assertiveness, and just
> getting that first step out of the house, really, when parents who
> have been stuck at home for five years and brought up the
> children, and the children are going to school or whatever, feel
> that they need to do something else but don't feel confident
> enough yet to make that first step into college.

A similar situation existed at the Big Wheel Nursery, where most of the mothers
were young, with a high proportion of teenage mothers. A lack of confidence to
approach the nursery's mother and toddler group among young mothers was
recognised and steps were taken to overcome it. As the manager explained:

> The girls find it hard to go to Mums and Toddlers' and sit round walls as
> mum and toddler groups often do because they feel they're [too] young …
> A lack of confidence, isn't it, to walk through that door … we offer
> transport. We'll go out and bring the girls into our groups originally so that
> they start to feel comfortable and then we'll offer them a course maybe …

The offer of transport for mothers and their children by staff of the Big Wheel was
the most direct way of getting parents to attend activities arranged by the nursery.
The aim of the nursery (or more specifically the project the nursery was a crucial
part of) was to get young women into the centre first and then to offer them
childcare while they attended a training course or completed their education,
building upon their newly found confidence. The examples of High Peaks and the
Big Wheel were similar to those at The Tree House and are described by participants

in Appendix 2. These examples also demonstrate the ways in which community nurseries can act to address lack of confidence among parents.

Helping parents to access education, training and employment

As already noted, many people of working age who are not in employment are pessimistic about getting a job because of a lack of skills and/or experience they feel employers require.[17] Community nurseries play an important role in overcoming such feelings because a significant proportion are involved in projects to help parents access education and training courses and employment. In the survey of community nurseries, for example, nearly half (43.4 per cent) the respondents said that they were part of projects aimed at helping parents into employment through education and/or training programmes. In other words, they directly provide services that help parents to access education, training and, eventually, employment. Several of the nurseries involved in the interviews were part of such projects. So, for example, in 1999, The Big Wheel opened a new education centre. The manager told a local paper (23 April 1999):

> The new centre will be delivering a whole programme of education and offering a range of courses, from basic skills through to GCSE and NVQ Levels ... We hope to encourage them [young mothers] to carry on with their education, providing practical and emotional support for them as well as free childcare.

At The Big Wheel Nursery the education courses were run in partnership with the local college, adult education service and careers office. At High Peaks, where parents could follow basic skills, IT and play work courses, funding came from the local college and the European Social Fund. In 1996/7 – 31 people attended training courses at High Peaks. The vast majority (27 people) managed to secure employment because of the training received at High Peaks. Their *Annual Report* shows how, in 1997, they provided a total of 701 training weeks. So at a very direct level community nurseries have the capacity to help parents into employment by improving the skills and experience that they are able to offer to employers.

Another way that community nurseries can help parents both to access and maintain employment is through offering affordable childcare places. In the mid-1990s, the price of a full time nursery place was estimated to be between £70 and £180 per week.[18] The average cost of £81.80 per week for full time childcare place for a child under two in the survey of community nurseries was at the lower end of those figures (Ackroyd Nursery quotes a figure of £107 per week). However, the majority (76.3 per cent) of the respondents in the survey noted that their nursery also charged at least one family subsidised fees. While no set model for the subsidisation of fees emerged from the research, such fees clearly gave substantial reductions on the costs of childcare. The average cost of a full time subsidised place for a child under two was £49.99 per week, 40 per cent lower than the full cost.

Even with the introduction of the Childcare Tax Credit, the provision of subsidised places is likely to remain important. This is because of two important shortcomings in the system. First, the proportion of fees that can be met is only 70 per cent of childcare. Second, the maximum amount upon which the 70 per cent can be charged is limited to £100 for one child and £150 for two or more children. However, the typical cost of a nursery place in England is £110 per week.[19] Hence parents eligible for Childcare Tax Credit, who are by definition lower paid, may have to find relatively substantial amounts to meet the shortfall between the Childcare Tax Credit and their childcare costs. For lower paid employees, for example, paying 30 per cent of £49.99 (£15.00) should be more manageable than paying 30 per cent of £81.80 (£24.54).

Some of the children of parents interviewed were in free childcare places while their parents attended training/educational courses. Those parents made it clear that without the free places they could not have pursued their studies or training. As Linda said at High Peaks:

> A lot of us did want to go to college. We went on taster sessions and a lot of us were interested in some of the courses there but the childcare up there… you've got to find £5.50 a day, but none of us could do that. But this is ESF [European Social Fund] funding where the childcare gets paid for which is a big help 'cos without that none of us would be able to afford the nursery. I've got two children and there's no way I could afford to pay for two children to go to crèche.

Five pounds 50 pence a day may sound a modest fee for childcare. However, Linda was receiving income support of only £67 per week. Hence, a day's childcare at the local college for her two children at a cost of £11 would have been almost a fifth of her weekly income support. Sheila at The Tree House Nursery also compared prices to the cost of childcare provided by the university she was attending:

> I wouldn't have actually been able to afford the college crèche.
> The college charges went up £5 last term so it would have been
> [an] extra £15 a week compared to what I pay here.

For many of the parents the cost of the childcare offered by their community nursery was one of the main factors in deciding to use the nursery. The views of Christian, 'It was the one we could afford' and Karen, 'I know that price-wise it [the nursery] compares very well with other ones', were typical.

Precarious survival: issues facing community nurseries

The commitment to providing affordable childcare has associated problems. The main issue is funding, in particular the difficulties involved in balancing the provision of high quality, yet affordable childcare. The ways in which that balance is obtained varied between the nurseries involved in the interviews. At one extreme, the manager of the Big Wheel explained how, in addition to the £60,000 it was given by the charity it is part of, it received:

> … other funding in the region of £125,000 … on a yearly basis. I
> get this from a SRB grant, Children in Need, joint finance which
> is health and social services money. Trusts, oil companies give me
> [funding]. The Church Urban Fund had just given us quite a
> large grant. Adult education pay for our classes.

At the other extreme, the Bridge Nursery was able to provide affordable fees for two main reasons. First, staff were poorly paid. Before the introduction of the national minimum wage, staff were paid £3.00 per hour except for the manager and her deputy who received £4.00 per hour. To meet the cost of the introduction of the national minimum wage, fees were increased from £1 per hour, a level it had been at for several years, to £1.25 per hour. Second, the nursery had high levels of support from parents and the wider community. So, for example, in the week before the interview, the nursery had raised £5,000 after its pre-school room was broken into and computer and electric equipment were stolen. The manager also described a barter system that the nursery operated, whereby parents were given free childcare places in return for the supply of certain goods (for example, carpets) or services (for example, plumbing).

These examples demonstrate the differences in funding possibilities for community nurseries. They highlight problems, particularly in the case of the Bridge. Low wages are common in childcare work and may present an obstacle to greater levels of qualification among staff (although it would be wrong to suggest that the Bridge Nursery had high levels of unqualified staff; in fact, all staff were qualified or working towards NVQ Level 2). And, despite current enthusiasm for local exchange trading schemes, there are obvious problems with providing childcare services dependent upon the informalities of barter-type systems. That said, there was little indication from the manager of the Bridge to suggest that she was concerned about the survival of the nursery. She had a powerful belief that the nursery would meet its commitments through the continued support of the community.

At the time of the research there was a feeling among exactly half the respondents to the survey that the financial situation of their nursery was insecure. It is somewhat paradoxical that concerns with funding often emerged where community nurseries were reliant upon more formal arrangements, particularly local authority funding. For those nurseries receiving funding from their local authority (three-quarters received such funding), there were specific issues about the inconsistent way in which their local authority made decisions regarding financial support. At the Castle the managers said:

> **Manager 1** I think it's down to the grant that it's [the nursery] insecure isn't it?
>
> **Manager 2** The grant used to be reviewed … three yearly and now it's reviewed yearly. And I know it got cut by … £500 this time which wasn't too bad. But the time before… they cut it by £3000. … with them reviewing it yearly you're always, like, waiting to know if they're going to cut it a lot or be generous, like just £500 this year. Well, it's still a cut but at least it wasn't by thousands and sometimes there is even a worry they're going take it away altogether.

Receiving local authority funding, therefore, is somewhat of a mixed blessing. While such funding is gratefully received, constant review and the possibility of cuts does not always make it a secure form of income. Where community nurseries are heavily dependent upon local authority funding, their existence arguably becomes inherently unstable as they are exposed to the vagaries of the relationships between local and central government. That is becoming clear in the relationship between the policies of the National Childcare Strategy and their effects at a local level. The example of the Tree House Nursery demonstrates the point.

The manager of the Tree House nursery felt funding for the nursery she received from the local authority was fairly secure but she worried about future funding arrangements:

> The city council are saying to us that they will be reviewing over the first six months of the Working Families' Tax Credit … our funding because if all parents are able to get the full amount through Working Families' Tax Credit then we've got to charge it to them. I feel certainly at the moment that it [the nursery] is secure … But I think it is always subject to constant monitoring … like with the Working Families'.

Anecdotal evidence suggests that many local authorities are considering reducing their commitment to community nurseries by emphasising the need for parents to claim Childcare Tax Credit and for community nurseries to see it as an intrinsic part of their revenue.[20] The Childcare Tax Credit is perhaps an even more unpredictable form of income than local authority grants. It is means-tested and, therefore, there is no guarantee that eligible parents will claim and receive it.

There is an additional problem in that, from September 1998 onwards, the Government guaranteed all four-year-olds a free place of two and a half hours a day in early years education in settings – private, state and voluntary – that meet Ofsted criteria. The survey was conducted in the summer of 1998 so respondents were asked if they thought this would affect their nursery. Over two-thirds (69.5 per cent) thought that the number of four-year-olds attending would fall. However, in interviews with nursery representatives which took place in the summer of 1999, it was not clear that this had actually happened. So, for example, the manager of the Barn nursery thought that they would lose a lot of children on the introduction of the guarantee of free early years places, but that had not happened because of:

> … a combination of two reasons. [First] the local schools didn't actually start providing for the younger fours like some schools in different parts of the borough. …[Second] once parents have been with us for quite some time they develop a degree of loyalty and appreciation for the fact that we do actually meet the needs of their children.

In contrast, the manager of High Peaks highlighted how local schools:

> Are taking them [children] earlier and earlier now and schools are taking them full time rather than part time. I think it was last

September [1998] we lost quite a few to the local primary school earlier than we would have done the year before, which makes it quite difficult for our pre-school room.

She went on to outline a nursery school drop-off service that had been developed by High Peaks to keep as many four-year-olds as possible for as much of the day as possible. The provision of this service was an attempt to meet the needs of both the parents and the nursery:

We try to be as supportive as possible. We do a nursery run. We'll pick children up at half eleven and bring them back here for lunch or take them at one o'clock for the afternoon session and pick them back up at half three so they can come back for their tea. That reduces their parents' fees quite a bit obviously 'cos there's that chunk missing out of the day. And it's also our security because we are keeping those children that bit longer.

The Bridge Nursery had taken a somewhat different approach to maintain numbers in the face of free early education places for four-year-olds. In order to encourage parents of four-year-olds to keep their children at the Bridge Nursery, they extended the number of free hours (four rather than just two and a half hours) offered.

The situation facing community nurseries is a good example of the policy contradictions which, as the OECD point out, affect all forms of early years provision. However, because of their precarious financial situation, community nurseries may well be harder hit than most.

The contribution of community nurseries to daycare provision

The discussion in this chapter has so far concentrated on the ways in which community nurseries help contribute to New Labour's aim of tackling social exclusion through integration into labour markets, and the policy contradictions inherent in such an approach. This section is concerned with the distinct contribution that community nurseries make to daycare provision.

There can be little doubt that the Government accepts that the vast majority of registered childcare will be provided by the private sector. For those children deemed to be 'in need', there may be access to local family support services. This could mean a social worker justifying a place in a family centre in order to avoid a child coming to harm. Family support has become stigmatised as moral arguments are used to condemn as failures the parents of children using such services.[21] With few exceptions, the children using family support will come from poor families who face a range of socio-economic problems and deprivations. Family support focuses on work both with children and their parents. This means that parents are not necessarily freed to pursue their own goals that may include education or paid employment. In contrast, they are expected to attend with their children to develop their parenting skills. The Government's Sure Start programme has aimed to develop such family support services in local communities.

At the other extreme, private nurseries are motivated by the need to make a profit. Hence they charge the highest price it is thought the market (parents looking for childcare) will pay. This means that privately provided childcare is exclusive to the children of those parents who can afford to pay market rates. This has an impact on the geography of private daycare provision, which tends to be concentrated in more prosperous areas, leaving more disadvantaged areas bereft of such provision.

Community nurseries exist somewhere between the two extremes of state-funded family support and private daycare provision. Their aim is to provide daycare at affordable prices for all parents. On the whole, the approach of community nurseries is more inclusive than that of both the state and market sectors. Because of the focus on children 'in need', state provision tends to exclude all but the very poorest, while private nurseries exclude all but the relatively well off. In contrast, community nurseries tend to take children from a whole range of socio-economic backgrounds. The Castle, for instance, had close contacts with social services with whom they had a service level agreement to take a number of children. These children played and learned alongside the children of fee-paying parents. The managers were pleased with that particular aspect of their nursery and explained:

> Lots of the children have really hard home lives. Lots of them may
> be seen as children in need. We work very closely with social
> services and with health visitors. We provide a much needed
> daycare service where the children receive education but also a level
> of care and [we] jointly work with social workers and health visitors,
> which I know they really value. We're quite unique in that respect.

In a period when different social groups are increasingly restricted to exclusive geographical areas[22], community nurseries offer a good example of how children from various social, economic and cultural backgrounds are able to play, learn and develop together. In this sense community nurseries are more egalitarian and democratic than other forms of daycare, particularly that which is provided by the private sector. The aim is to provide services for children, and often their parents, no matter what their background.[23] As the manager of the Bridge succinctly put it: 'My main aim is to be here for whoever crosses that door.' What she meant was that she aimed to meet the needs – not necessarily just childcare – of those children and parents who approached her nursery. The manager of High Peaks spoke in more depth about such issues:

> It's about being there for the community … It's identifying their needs and trying to work to what the community needs in order to support them whether it be training, childcare, personal or social problems. It's being there. It's being open and flexible and being able to recognise when some of the parents that we do see need that extra bit of support or need that extra bit of help for whatever reason. I think High Peaks is probably more adaptable to that rather than the private sector nurseries that probably wouldn't be able to identify those needs and probably only see the parents for five minutes in the morning and five minutes in the evening.

The manager of High Peaks comments usefully summarise the distinctiveness of community nurseries. Such nurseries are able to cater for the needs of local people because they are not in the business of making a profit. This enables them to engage with the needs – 'whether it be training, childcare, personal or social problems' – of local people. Beyond childcare, private nurseries are unable to engage with such issues because, in the final analysis, they are there to make a profit, not to engage with apparently extraneous activities such as meeting the broader social and economic needs of local people.

Other managers of community nurseries also felt their nurseries to be different from those in the private sector. The managers of the Castle, for example, highlighted how being a not-for-profit nursery created a perception with the public that their nursery was more child-centred:

> **Manager 1** It means a lot because we're not a profit-making nursery. We're not here for the money. We are here to provide.
> Interviewer: Do you think that makes a difference to the way the nursery is run?
> **Manager 2** It makes a difference to the way it's run and it makes a difference to people's impressions of the place. They'll think 'Oh well, they're not here just to cream all the money off. They're actually here for the children.'

Their view was supported by the parents of children attending the Castle. For example, Sally, whose daughter attended, spoke about her experiences of visiting local private nurseries:

> I mean we went to look round the others [private nurseries]. They almost ignored Milly [Sally's daughter] ... they were sort of just talking to me as a visitor, but as soon as I came [to the Castle] it was though Milly came in first. They got down on her level and they were talking to her and showing her everything. And she responded to them whereas because she was totally ignored at the other places we went to, it was as though she didn't matter. It was as though all they really wanted was my money ... they weren't concerned about my child.

It could be that Sally just had a bad experience. After all, if private nurseries are to make a profit they will surely be aware of ways to make parents, through their children, keen on their services. However, other parents made similar observations. Describing the Bridge nursery, for example, Mandy said: 'I like the family atmosphere ... I mean they care about the children. Instead of caring about who's paying what, they actually care about the children'. Nigel, whose son also attended the Tree House noted:

> I know they [the Tree House] have to ... break even and keep afloat, but it takes away that thing, the bottom line business thing. It doesn't mean they're forever just looking at the bottom line 'cos they get funding from various places ... and it makes it more thinking of the child's welfare as opposed to the bank balance.

Conclusion

Our study of community nurseries suggests that their main aim is to provide accessible, affordable childcare for parents, where more often than not, it was lacking or absent. The extent to which this focus has departed from the original sentiments of the community nurseries movement is debatable. There certainly still exists a commitment to equality and giving parents access to activities such as paid employment and education. In many nurseries there is still a commitment to providing for local children and their families, although this is often part of a requirement of funding arrangements. There is also a commitment in many community nurseries to providing services for the wider local community and not just the parents of children attending the nursery.

However, at the more ideological level of collective organisation and problem resolution, there has been a clear departure. There was, for example, no indication that community nurseries are now in the business of challenging the process of professionalisation. While parents continue to be involved in management committees, there were clearly difficulties involved in this, particularly finding parents with the skills now required to manage a community nursery. Many of the nurseries were equivalent to small businesses, with turnovers of hundreds of thousands of pounds. It is difficult to envisage, particularly in the current climate of prudence in public finances and the demand for accountability, how community nurseries could survive without the input of a range of professionals. Indeed, the whole childcare sector is now so closely regulated it is not easy to envisage challenges to the status quo without the risk of losing status as care and/or education providers.

Community nurseries now face a new set of challenges and dilemmas. For example, we have seen that local authorities are examining the core funding they give many community nurseries and transferring it from direct service support to users through the Working Families' Tax Credit. Community nurseries have had to face the loss of four-year-olds (and increasingly three-year-olds) to pre-school classes (particularly those attached to primary schools) and nursery classes. Some of the nurseries featured in this chapter have proved resilient, with the support of their local community, to such challenges in the past. The most immediate issue is whether this resilience can be maintained. It would be ironic, given the fact that community nurseries are able to deliver services in many of the Government's priority areas, such as childcare in disadvantaged communities and the tackling of social exclusion through education, training and employment programmes if this was not the case.

Despite all the rhetoric of 'partnership' and 'choice', the provision of daycare remains essentially market-led. It remains unclear as to whether the new neighbourhood nurseries initiative, particularly in the long term, will be able to provide services for parents whose spending power is limited because of low incomes. Community nurseries have a valuable role to play in the provision of such services, which often go beyond the provision of childcare. The real question is how to frame and implement policies that we can draw on something to which we return to in the concluding chapter.

4 Case study one –
Ackroyd Under Fives Nursery

Ackroyd community nursery is located within a large old building that is used as a local community centre. The community centre serves rows of terraced streets and, slightly further afield, a council estate, now part-privatised and rented out by private landlords. The community centre is multi-purpose and used seven days a week, from 8am to 10pm. It caters for around 26 groups, including the nursery, an elderly citizens' project, an out-of-school club and a local Evangelist church. The downstairs facilities include a kitchen/dining room and a large hall, plus a small garden.

Ackroyd was started by a group of local women who were unhappy with the regimes at the local council nurseries and concerned about the lack of facilities for working mothers in the area. After much lobbying, they obtained an urban aid grant and opened in 1980 for 15 children aged 18 months to five years. In 1984, the nursery persuaded the council to purchase a terraced house a few doors down from the community centre and, with an additional grant from the GLC, it was opened as a baby unit for six children. Further grants enabled more expansion to take place. The nursery now offers the equivalent of 34 full-time places for children aged two to four, and 12 places for babies.

As well as being part of a building where there are many things going on, Ackroyd Nursery is rooted in its local community. The coordinator also lives down the street and the children attending the nursery visit her home or the local shops or park; and various friends and older children drop into the nursery. The pensioner who lives next door to the baby unit does her washing in the baby unit laundry room and pops in for a cup of tea when she is lonely.

The coordinator and some of the management committee have been partly involved with the nursery since it began nearly 20 years ago. In the account that follows, they reflect on the ups and downs they have encountered in trying to keep the nursery going despite cutbacks in grants, changes of funding regimes and new rules and regulations which continually challenge their considered, but relaxed and informal, friendly, neighbourhood approach.

Reflections on how we have survived

Solid foundations

In the beginning we had to work very hard to justify a grant. We did research into community nurseries, we learnt from the experiences of others, we tried to document local needs. We put forward a coherent picture of what was needed and of the kind of vision we had for the nursery. We have made changes, of course, but that initial vision has stayed with us.

Ethos and practice of community ownership

- We are convinced that everyone in the nursery and in the immediate neighbourhood served by the community centre should have a say in what the nursery does. We have written it into our structure. We have equal numbers of parents/staff/other local residents on the management committee, who make all the important decisions about the nursery. We have maintained this management committee structure, even though our constitution has been amended to allow for minor but necessary changes, and despite pressures to do otherwise. We've even been prepared to argue with the Charity Commission, rather than compromise this principle.
- We are based in a multifunctional community centre – the opportunities to engage with other local people and other users of the community centre are very important to us. There is community rapport – we join in with activities in the community centre.
- We know the local community inside out. We have active links to local schools, to health centres, to the women's refuge and so on. We are available to them and we expect that they, in turn, will support us.
- We are local. All children live within half a mile radius.
- The parents' group was set up by the parent representatives of the management committee. They meet regularly, discuss nursery policies and procedures, and organise a social fund and social events.
- Staff also come from the local area – we have a deliberate policy to employ local people, especially parents.
- We are sympathetic to family needs far beyond the provision of childcare. Some of the things we have done include: fundraising for a terminally ill parent to visit her homeland; organising a babysitting rota for children while Mum was in hospital having another child, in order to prevent her children going into temporary care; transporting children to/from nursery because parents are

disabled or are unable to bring children themselves; assisted an asylum seeker's family to cope with the loss of their child through cot death, including raising money for funeral expenses and making arrangements. We have an open door approach – we try to help with any problems brought to us, for example, problematic relationships or finding temporary accommodation. Our policy is never to turn anyone away who is in need of help.[1]

■ The nursery serves a cross section of the community, for example, a mix of class, ages, sex/gender and racial background, ability and disability.

Community empowerment is a fundamental concept underlying our provision. We have found ways to involve everyone. We utilise people's skills/knowledge on the management committee and in the day-to-day running of activities. We describe ourselves as professional in terms of the quality of the service we offer, but we are not aloof like some highly professionalised services. Parents (and children) comment on the friendliness and welcoming atmosphere. There is strong leadership and a sense of commitment within the staff and management group. There has been the same Coordinator and Deputy Coordinator for 20 years and most of the staff team have been with us over 14 years. This means that there is a strong sense of trust within the staff team and management body. People – parents as well as staff – have stayed involved over long periods. Everyone is willing to do a bit extra, for example, staff help out when the cook is ill, local people come in, too. We have *never* had to employ agency staff to cover vacancies, maternity leave, etc.

The child's needs come first

Our open to all approach on a first come, first served basis is achieved by a sliding scale of fees (presently seven bands; from a minimum fee of £32.50 to £107.50 per week, plus two free places for students/asylum seekers). We also accept seven children at risk through social services. We offer full and part time places. There is continuity of care in familiar surroundings, for example, from the baby unit to the nursery, and from the nursery to after-school club and play schemes. (Note: we now need a youth club!). Some of the children who went to the nursery as children are now parents themselves with children in the nursery. Over the years we introduced add-on services, for example, a toy library and parent/toddler groups in order to provide a range of services under one roof for parents with different needs (working parents and parents at home).

The nursery offers an innovative 'shared-care' arrangement with local schools for four-year-olds. Children are gradually introduced into the school environment, which means their move from nursery to school is not an abrupt change but a more pleasant experience. This arrangement gives the nursery the space to offer part time places during the morning, usually allocated to local children who have no spoken English.

We want young children to be valued and to join in our local community. We have worked towards achieving government learning targets and we have become an eligible Ofsted provider. But we wish we could 'let children be' and have fun and not impose so much on them whilst they are so young.

Keeping going

We believe in offering a service to local people, whether or not they can afford it. Because our income does not match our costs, we have been dependent on annually reviewed grants. Last year we received a grant of £184,484 from the council, which included the nursery education grant. Our staff and other costs amount to £285,000. So we must raise the rest through our complicated fee structure and fundraising.

At present the local council pays some of our salary bill (but not enough – some of us have not had a pay rise for many years). We have had to learn how to lobby very hard to maintain our grant income – it has often been threatened. We have active links to local councillors and our local MP supports us. We work to maintain our profile. We have become used to making an annual lobby against cuts when grants come up for yearly reviews, to making presentations to councillors and to petitioning for childcare/voluntary sector provision. We see ourselves as part of the voluntary sector in the borough. We have recently begun to make links with the EYDCP.

We survived the loss of funding several times. The demise of the GLC Women's Committee hit us hard. We took cuts from the council – we lost our toy library funding. There was a hostile external environment and changes in public policy/public funding in the mid-90s, and all voluntary sector and childcare services suffered. It has got a little better, but not enough to survive without real effort. We have tried to attract new resources through fundraising to charitable trusts and local efforts to buy new toys. We have had to make internal changes, for example, annual staff employment contracts for approximately five years.

Coping with these external changes is not only a matter of coping with funding. We have been under great pressure to become an education provider. We have had to weigh the carrot of extra resources against dealing with increased bureaucracy of writing reports and case notes. We want our staff to take full advantage of local training, but we must pay the hidden costs, for example, funding to cover for staff attending training.

But we do have a real sense of achievement – we celebrate our history and we have a sense of pride in being involved in our community and in being a guide to others who have come to ask our advice.

We didn't give up.

5 Case study two –
Robert Owen Early Years Centre: Continuity and change

The Robert Owen Early Years Centre is in Greenwich, London. It is a Centre of Early Excellence and is mentioned as an example of a neighbourhood nursery in the DfES pamphlet[1] that announced the Neighbourhood Nursery Initiative.

Robert Owen has a long history. There were originally two state nursery schools on one site, Trafalgar and Conley Street, which were opened in the Second World War. Like so many other nursery schools, they were located in Horsa Huts, prefabricated buildings erected in the 1940s. The nursery schools opened to take children aged two to five, while their mothers were working in factories in London. They had 100 full time places between them and offered a long day, 8am to 5pm, to cover factory hours. The children had meals and regular health inspections and the two nursery schools hosted various fetes and community days. Everything was free, funded through the education system, and run by nursery head teachers, assisted by teachers and nursery nurses. The schools were much respected by the local community as a good local service. The nursery retains a record book of photos and press cuttings illustrating some of the events that took place and the public comments made about the nursery.

Gradually the service was whittled away as government policy changed. Conley Street Day Nursery became Robert Owen Nursery School and, from the 1960s, offered part time rather than full time places. The two schools amalgamated in the 1970s and the focus was on part time (two and a half hours), rather than full time education, although a limited number of full time places were available for older children or those deemed to be 'at risk'. The hours were reduced to the school day and school terms. The age range of the children was reduced, from two to five to three to four, with most of the four-year-olds leaving early to go to school. Yet at the same time as Robert Owen was offering a limited service, many local parents were paying for very expensive private nursery care.

Robert Owen was in a building that was near the end of its life. The accommodation was increasingly cramped, although the outside area was good and had both grass and tarmac spaces, wildlife areas and vegetable gardens. The local community, from having been predominantly white working-class, was now socially and ethnically mixed. Its catchment area included many streets of terraced houses, some of which had been renovated and sold on to young middle-class couples. It also included some very run-down and unpopular council estates. Mothers and fathers using the nursery asked staff for much more than the nursery could provide. There was also a considerable demand for childcare for a wider age range of children.

Robert Owen had one asset. It was very near the site for the Millennium Dome and the council had considerable regeneration money for the area. At an open consultation meeting, parents and other local people were clear that they wished to see Robert Owen Nursery School rebuilt. However, they were also clear that they did not wish to see it rebuilt in its current form. They argued for a nursery which took babies up to primary school at age five, somewhere that was open from 8am till 6pm, longer if possible, throughout the year.

In the series of meetings that followed, it became clear that there was also a demand for a community facility within the new nursery. A small group, the head teacher, the nursery inspector for the borough and the lead officer for early years in the chief executive's office, supported by outside consultants, including an architect, worked on translating stated – and sometimes unstated – ideas into concrete proposals. One such proposal was about offering support to less confident parents. Many of the mothers were not able to cope with the job market without support and preparation. They lacked qualifications, they had low self-esteem and there was a high rate of teenage pregnancies. They were people who did not feel they would be valued or wanted in the work place.

> We wanted to offer somewhere that you could go just because you're having a downer day, not because you need it five days a week, not because you even want it part time, but because it was a lousy day. It was raining. You were in your flat and you didn't have a place anywhere. You may be on 10 waiting lists, but you didn't actually have a place anywhere. We wanted somewhere that you could walk through the door and someone would say 'hiya', how are you …?

These ideas were tested with parent and staff groups and, where possible, directly with children themselves. They were also presented to senior council officers for further support. Whilst the parents and staff groups were generally supportive, there were many difficulties within the council about dovetailing plans and financing with other departments. The process of negotiation took more than four years before the building even began, leading to some disillusion amongst supporters.

In the end the money was forthcoming, both capital (over one million pounds) and revenue increased (the existing nursery school budget was expanded). The building, whose design had been so closely argued, opened this year (2001). It offers integrated care and education for children aged one to rising five in a separate nursery wing, which has smart-card security for safety. In the rest of the building, there are facilities for the local community and the wider childcare community.

The children are offered continuous care and education, staying in their home group, and their homeroom, with the same group of staff. All staff work flexible shifts, including the head teacher. Renegotiating traditional hours of work also presented some difficulties. Some of the new staff are unqualified local people who are working for their qualifications on site, taking advantage of the training facilities which are part of the wider centre.

Is the project working?

The nursery, although it does so much, also represents a series of compromises. The financing meant that there were compromises over the building. Although very serviceable, it was not state-of-the-art as originally intended. Some of the facilities for the youngest children were more expensive and more elaborate than was intended, because of the insistence of local registration officers. The centre wanted to take babies but the council for various reasons decided that children under the age of one ought to be at home or with a registered childminder. This is now causing great conflict with new parents who are returning to work from maternity leave. The restrictive size of the site meant the loss of wonderful outside areas, sacrificed for car parking and site access.

There are also unresolved budgetary issues. Three- and four-year-olds are funded for their nursery entitlement, as with any other education provider. But there is a funding issue for the one- to two-year-olds and for the childcare over and above the nursery education entitlement. There are one-year-olds and two-year-olds in part time and full daycare, and three and four-year-olds, some of whom are part time, but others who are on site from 8am until 6pm throughout the year. There is a scaled fee system, so people pay according to income and there is a two-year cushion to get started. Within three years, the nursery must be economically viable, the same as any other in the private or voluntary sector.

> It's means tested, but it's available for everyone. So if you're on
> income support, places are free. If you're on income of over
> £25,000 after tax, an 8am to 6pm place, five days a week, is £125,
> and that's comparable to what that income bracket would be
> paying in local day nurseries. For the parent who's just fed-up in
> their flat and wants to join us a couple mornings a week, it would
> cost £2 per session. We also run a drop-in centre and toddler and
> baby groups at a token charge.

The nursery has gone for economy of size. It could not afford to be small and still
be able to offer the range of local community opportunities it aimed for. It was in
any case obliged to keep the nursery school provision at its core. There are 142
equivalent full time places on site. The children are age grouped and will keep to
their group as they progress through the nursery. Eighteen of these places are for
one-year-olds (in two groups of nine). Twenty-four of the places are for two-year-olds
(also in two groups). There are 100 places for three- and four-year-olds, because that
was the size of the previous school. There is a requirement for some continuity of
attendance. Three and four-year-olds obviously have to attend morning or afternoon
every day in school terms, but may stay longer. One- and two-year-olds are required
to cross the threshold at least three times during the week. So within those
parameters we have a flexible system to meet parents' needs. Some children are
there between 8am and 6pm five days a week, 52 weeks a year. Others maybe come
on a Monday, Wednesday and Friday morning. Some children are there full time
from 8am until 6pm, but only on Monday, Tuesday and Wednesday, because of their
parents' working patterns. Flexibility is a priority for the organisation.

> We do our best to meet everybody's individual needs as they go
> through the centre. So throughout the course of the week, we
> actually serve over 300 families now.

Other facilities include a café with free Internet facilities, which is open to the whole
community and is well used. In the first six months, there were four Saturday open
days, which were well publicised and well attended. Some of the interest came from
local secondary school children who originally came from the nursery school. They
have started up their own after-school homework club in the café. Eight of them
come in after school and do their homework together, having a drink while they're
doing it.

There are rooms for EYDCP meetings, a variety of local voluntary and community
groups meet there, and there is a training suite. The Greenwich Portage Service and
Parent Partnership Officers are also based there.

> We have got a training room, a huge training room, which is used by professionals and by parents. Our Parents' Learning Centre starts soon. We've spent a lot of time doing questionnaires saying, 'What do you want? You said you wanted courses, put your money where your mouth is. What courses do you want?' We're actually kicking off with computer courses, because you can't get a job in an office nowadays unless you can work a computer. We're doing assertiveness courses. We're doing confidence-building courses. We're doing family literacy to help those who missed out on school, for whatever reason. Family numeracy for the same reason. We're also doing some baby massage and parenting skills. How to say 'no' to your two-year-old has proved one of the most popular ones.

As ever, the morality and practicalities of funding must be dealt with.

> We can't afford to provide staff just to talk through issues with parents, much as we would like to. Some of the courses we're having to make a slight charge for, but everybody is entitled to the government £150 individual learning grant. So, we're actually assisting parents to access that money. You can give (or take) everything for free, but does that make you feel better? Do parents actually want to feel that they're contributing? Accessing that money for them, so that people can pay us a small amount, may be useful all round. At least people feel this isn't charity. This is something that they are contributing to.

Robert Owen has a management committee. As a school it has always had a governing body. Fortunately, the governing body was mainly made up of parents. The two local authority governors who were on the governing body were former parents of children at the nursery. This arrangement was simply transferred to the new management committee. The governing body and the management committee have the same membership and meet at the same time, so that although notionally they are separate, as the education legislation requires, in practice they are exactly the same.

> We always had parent governors, but where we had to have a local business governor, we had a parent. Where we had to have a community governor, oh yes, that was a parent. So parents have always been very involved in everything. In the new management structure for the new facility we managed to keep the same

proportions, so we have three parent representatives. We have still got a community governor. We've still got a local business governor. We've still got two local authority reps. We've also widened the group, so we also have a health visitor from our local health centre and a representative from the local college who advises on courses.

Robert Owen was a nursery school and good nursery education is still at the heart of what goes on. It is still nominally a nursery school, but the administrative edges have been blurred in order to achieve continuity for children and community involvement. With imagination, the age-old distinctions between care and education, professionalism and community can be overcome. Nursery schools have a very strong tradition and the example of Robert Owen shows how it is possible to incorporate the strengths of the nursery education system and yet become a very different sort of neighbourhood organisation.

6 Case study three –
Marcus Garvey Nursery:
Catering for the black community

Introduction

This chapter discusses the Marcus Garvey Nursery[1] as a service provider to the local, black[2] community in Handsworth, Birmingham[3] in which the nursery is situated. The chapter discusses the role that Marcus Garvey plays in the community; the philosophy that provided the basis for the nursery's origins and its operation over 25 years; the discrimination experienced by workers and parents; and the nursery's relationship with professionals in mainstream organisations, namely local government and primary schools.

In this chapter 'community' refers to, first, the children who have attended and who are still attending the nursery; second, the parents of those children and the workers in the nursery; and third, the residents who live in the area in which the nursery is situated. Since Marcus Garvey was set up and continues to cater for the local black community, it is best regarded as a 'community' nursery. It encapsulates the idea of partnership (between local residents and organisations) and has adopted the community education notion of learning through social movements or social involvement.[4, 5] At Marcus Garvey this has meant a focus upon black culture, history and identity.

Researching Marcus Garvey Nursery

The chapter originates from small-scale research over nine months, in which we investigated the overall success of Marcus Garvey Nursery in the year 2000[6]. We reviewed literature relating to early years in general and community nursery more specifically. We conducted 15 in-depth individual and group interviews with past and present parents, people who had attended the nursery as children, and nursery workers. Group interviews comprised between three and seven persons. We collected fieldnotes of our nursery observations, telephone conversations and discussions between various professionals involved in early years and childcare. Furthermore, we collected diary entries of testimonials and/or stories told by participants at a recent workshop on community nurseries in November 2000.

About Marcus Garvey Nursery

Origins and development

Marcus Garvey was established as a community nursery in October 1976 with Syble Morgan, a Jamaican immigrant, as the first head. The nursery was set up from adaptations of similar provisions Syble Morgan observed during several previous visits to the USA. The nursery belongs to a wider organisation, the Harambee Organisation Ltd, West Midlands. Harambee not only set up the original Marcus Garvey Nursery and still owns it, but also created and owns other services such as a housing association, a welfare rights advice centre, a mental health and counselling centre and a bookshop. All but the housing association began after Marcus Garvey was established. Since 1970, Harambee has had a policy-making, entrepreneurial and management function. All its staff are black.

Marcus Garvey nursery is located in a three-storey, mid-terrace, Georgian house situated on a long inner-city backstreet. It was organised at a time when racial tension was rife in British inner cities generally, and Birmingham in particular,[7] and in a period when under-fives provision in Handsworth was patchy, of poor quality, poorly managed and often domestic, that is mainly childminding, and unregulated. It was also at a time when it was believed that state-provided nurseries in Handsworth discriminated against black children by refusing to offer them nursery education, or, if black children were admitted, by failing to meet the children's and the parents' cultural needs. Apart from the account by the Community Relations Commission,[8] the full extent of discrimination is unknown. However, various parents and workers of Marcus Garvey recall persistent refusal in the 1970s when attempting to access mainstream nurseries as demonstrated by a parent:

> **Parent** Black people didn't have a nursery to send their kids.
> **Interviewer** Was that because they were rejected from the mainstream?
> **Parent** Yes they were. So this is where this organisation come in for black kids.

This should be of little surprise given the fact that many studies have shown how black children are failed in the education system in Britain.[9, 10, 11, 12]

Marcus Garvey Nursery therefore sought, and continues to seek, to:

- focus on black, African-Caribbean philosophy and awareness which can be reflected in practice;
- meet the cultural and social needs of the children who attend. This is mirrored through the nursery's day-to-day focus on black culture and identity in all its pursuits such as black play activities and the provision of African-Caribbean food. It is hoped that this early cultural input and focus on positive discriminatory practices would better prepare black children for later life through combating educational underachievement and social exclusion;
- provide full daycare from 7.30am to 6.30pm for 40 children aged between two to four and to provide pre-school education that would include bilingualism;
- provide training and support for African-Caribbean parents, especially in parental skills;
- employ an all black workforce at all levels from management to ancillary staff;
- provide a homely, culturally-sensitive environment in which the local community can socialise.

Syble Morgan summarises the aims of setting up the nursery. It was to be:

> … accountable to us, black people in the community, to determine our own needs and to set our own policies for meeting those needs. …It is important to note here that although our management committee and our staff are black, we have had white children at our nursery.[13]

The aims have not changed significantly over the years. In relation to the needs of black people in the area, the present head notes that, 'our aims and our objectives [are] to build self-esteem of black children and to encourage parents to go back to work'.

Today there are other black-led, community nurseries in Handsworth. However, unlike Marcus Garvey Nursery, they were not set up primarily to serve the black community *per se* but the local community. The workforce at these other nurseries is mainly black and the children and parents who attend are predominantly black, too. Nonetheless, the significant proportion of black 'presence' at these other nurseries can be explained by the large proportion of black residents in the catchment area and, furthermore, the black people who attend, generally comprise of a mix of ethnic groups from the locality rather than only of African-Caribbean origin. In the sense that Marcus Garvey has deliberately set out to cater exclusively for the African-Caribbean community, although other ethnic groups are also welcomed, it is one of only a few nurseries with the specific focus on services for African-Caribbean children and parents.

Discrimination and survival

A notable attribute of Marcus Garvey as a black organisation is its ability to function and provide day-to-day service for 25 years as a community nursery amid racial discrimination. In its early days, Marcus Garvey experienced funding constraints due to racial discrimination by funders. This financial restraint was in addition to the lack of funds in community nurseries[14] and childcare more generally[15] and deep cuts in social policy provision because of economic and political changes since the 1970s.[16, 17] At Marcus Garvey, discrimination came especially from local government in Birmingham and mainstream feeder primary schools:

> **Syble Morgan** I can remember when they [funders] wouldn't sign the cheques if they heard that we were only catering for the black community.

> **Former assistant head** There was a lot of uncertainty about funding and I think that [name of funder] withdrew in 1982 and there was a lot of grumbling about how we were being funded.

> **Nursery officer** As soon as they find out that it is a black organisation, the schools don't want to work with us.

In discussions with the present head, it would seem that the relationship between black and white organisations or, at least Marcus Garvey Nursery and local government in terms of funding, has greatly improved since the 1970s.

> **Interviewer** And they've never withdrawn funding or anything like that?

> **Head** Oh no!

> **Interviewer** So things have changed over time … [Others have] mentioned that in the early days when they first started, the Council would, at times, withdraw funds and all the other funders, when they realised that it was black.

> **Head** Really?… News to me. No, I didn't know that.

Despite the opposition that the nursery experienced in its early years, it has weathered the storm and things have slowly improved.

Besides the funding issue, the nursery's ability to survive over many years is all the more poignant given that, at the beginning, members of the committee were unqualified for, and inexperienced in, the task of setting-up and running *any* organisation:

> **Former member** When you start something in Birmingham where you have no blacks in any position of management, no position of authority, no position of qualifications, limited qualifications, such as the nursery, you know, but limited, you are bringing people together who are unskilled …

> **Former head** And unskilled that's running the organisation …(laughter) … and you know what you want the organisation to do … And with the determination that it is going to work whatever happens. Whatever skills we didn't have, we were either going to acquire it, or do it the way we think it ought to be done, but it was going to get done and it did get done.

In conversation, former committee members, who are all now highly qualified professionals, give vivid accounts of horrendous business meetings:

> **Former member** Can you imagine, the meeting start at 6.30 in the evening …

> **Former head** Awful, awful those things were …

> **Former member** And the meeting finish at 12 o'clock [midnight].

> **Former head** Everybody was there … whatever might be not going as good as we wanted it, was discussed … They [meetings] were a laugh. Everything was thrashed out. We never get up until the agenda finished.

> **Parent** Oh yeah, that would take a long time.

This lack of experience in conducting business to achieve the effective management of the nursery was short-lived. Some of the original team members still serve on the committee although most have left and have been replaced by new members.

> **Former member** It's simple now because you are now educated and it is part of the system.

> **Head** Coming later to the system, the committee now is pure
> professionals.

Meetings are now run in a more skilled and proficient manner. Whereas the original committee were suspicious of professionals since, for them professionals consisted of white racists, it now consists of all black professionals. The pendulum has swung in the other direction, which has had detrimental repercussions for local parents and community residents. Unskilled local people are now excluded from the decision-making process; only skilled parents are represented. However, as pointed out in Chapter 2, the business management demands of community nurseries now justify a professional committee. Nonetheless, despite the lack of management skills for former committee members, it needs to be acknowledged that they preserved the zealousness and confidence that has meant the nursery has survived as a service provider for the black community for 25 years.

Catering for African-Caribbean children

One of the most notable differences between Marcus Garvey Nursery and other nurseries is its provision for children of African-Caribbean origin. A significant difference here is its deliberate and conscientious attempt to not only educate the children in preparation for school, but also to integrate this education with a strong awareness of self as a black person in preparation for life in the wider world. The research produced many accounts where parents chose the nursery over the other nurseries in the locality for cultural and identity reasons:

> What I liked about the nursery especially for my children, was
> the teaching aspect – getting them prepared and ready for
> school … My children went through the Marcus Garvey Nursery.
> I've got three children and all three of them have gone through
> the system. My last child, I was living in Cheshire but I made sure
> that I brought him all the way back to Birmingham for him to
> actually go through that system because it worked really well for
> my other two children … for my child, it was having the role
> models, having all the black workers there for them to see, for
> my child to see that, you know, we can work at different levels as
> cooks, cleaners, managers, the lot. So it was very positive for us.
> Also it was about the teaching aspects as well. They were being

taught about their heritage. Also surviving and also looking at the education system, so there were a lot of things that was being taught within the nursery.
(Mother whose, now adult, children attended the Marcus Garvey Nursery)

One of my children went there ... [it] is [also] about children seeing black people in a positive way. Mixing with other black people and enjoying being with other black people. Sometimes you send them to a city council nursery and all they see are white people in positions of authority and again when they go to school this is also the norm ... It is not just about the academic stuff but I think the emphasis was about children having a very good grounding regarding their identity which would then enhance whatever they then did in life. Because even though children were leaving at three and four, to give them that kind of input, even if it is just for a year, assisted them in later life. There were issues that they were able to focus on such as how they were received into school, because sometimes the teachers basically couldn't believe it when parents went in and said my child can read and write. And I think one of the things we did was the basic A, B, C ... We did phonics as well because we wanted to give the children the widest experience as possible so that they weren't going into school with just A, B, C and not knowing what the sounds were. It helped and it worked. I know at the school that one of my children go to there were children from the Marcus Garvey nursery attended there as well.
(Mother 2 whose, now adult, child attended Marcus Garvey Nursery)

I wanted my daughter to go here because, one, I wanted her to go to school amongst African-Caribbean children. Secondly, I wanted her to understand and be grounded firmly in her culture and her roots. And I think this here nursery offers that. And also, it has made her very confident. So there's a lot of things about her personality that I think the nursery has enhanced and made stronger.
(Father whose primary school age child previously went to Marcus Garvey Nursery)

The nursery's aims of instilling a sense of black cultural identity in their children is met in several ways: through its staff composition, the educational materials used, such as books, nursery rhymes, toys, pictures and posters, food and the celebration of cultural festivals. The father, mentioned earlier, describes his observations of the nursery:

> Looking behind, that is the spider, but I'm sure it's taken more
> from Annancy than you know, your everyday European aspect of
> 'hincy-wince spider'… I mean, I understand that 'hincy, wince
> spider', but you know, I think, that can be used in a lot of other
> ways developing the Annancy stories[18] … The graduation[19] is
> done in a very African-centered way. They celebrate Quansar,
> which is a very African-centered festival … There's nothing about
> the nursery that I would say that's European … most of the
> books and stuff and pictures of people and even looking around
> now, I'm trying to see pictures of a white child really, and I can't
> see one. So, not to say, they shouldn't be, but it's a big contrast
> when you compare it to nurseries where you don't see no black
> children. You see pure, … white children …

Although black ideology is apparent in a practical way throughout the nursery, we discovered that it has changed over time. In its early years the Marcus Garvey Nursery had an ideaology of separatism that focused exclusively on accepting Caribbean/Jamaican culture and which actively rejected other cultures in an act of positive discrimination.[20, 21] However, there has been a definite shift towards multiculturalism, defined here as not only promoting one's own identity but also embracing an awareness and appreciation of cultural alternatives. This change of ethos is often noticed by staff and parents returning to visit the nursery after many years of absence:

> A former manager of Harambee … stated while looking around
> the room at the pictures on the walls and other play equipment,
> 'You haven't made your mark, Collette [directed to the present
> Head] or have you? Collette replied by saying that she was
> oblivious to the nursery's former physical appearance and has
> attempted to design it in a way that she thinks will be pleasing to
> parents and children alike, acceptable to her and to her staff.
>
> *(Fieldnotes)*

The present head feels that this shift in ideology is warranted to reflect, represent and keep in step with the current thinking and beliefs of young black people:

> In the first few years we've been talking about the black heroes more so, whereas now it's us and identity. I don't think parents are saying so much, you know, 'You haven't taught them about Queen Nzinga and you haven't taught them about … the ancient black heroes'. And I'm sure it's the fact that things are changing in England. Like there's more on the telly. There's more books. There's more toys, and there's more dolls. And as I said, the knowledge and the imputs going on at home. So that when they come here the expectation's not so strong … it's about three years ago we were thinking, started to drop a strong black focus ourselves as well. You know, just use our basic stuff, like make sure that … they're painting their faces, because we do that a lot. I don't think a child can go through the nursery at all before having that experience of talking about themselves, painting themselves.

The educational and cultural input acquired at Marcus Garvey Nursery seem to have paid off in terms of the concrete and anecdotal evidence of educational and employment success of the children who attended.

> **Former pupil 1** We look at the nursery that started 20 years ago and we can say, yes we have made it [completed a University degree]. We haven't given into peer pressure. It can be done.

> **Former pupil 2** Well, I'm a nursery nurse and I work at Marcus Garvey Day Nursery, Monday to Friday, go to college on a Wednesday, completing my NVQ Level 2 in early years …
> **Interviewer** you attended the Marcus Garvey Nursery … when you were about two or three?
> **Former pupil 2** Yeah …
> **Interviewer** Did any of your friends attend Marcus Garvey Nursery?
> **Former pupil 2** Yeah.
> **Interviewer** How many?
> **Former pupil 2** Quite a lot actually.
> **Interviewer** What are they doing now?
> **Former pupil 2** Two of them are doing Business Administration.

Couple of them are doing health and social care … leisure and tourism, hair and beauty.

Mother 1 My daughter, she is now teaching, primary school children. And my son he works for a finance company.

Assistant head Princess is at UCE [University of Central England] doing a nursing degree. I saw her … And Lloyd who went to become a model … And there is also Bobby and Jamie, you know the gentleman who is a pharmacist … And Patrick. So there is so much …

Nursery officer And Rexroy is designing … The preacher man … with his two sons Kenneth and, I can't remember, they are doing quite well as well.

Mother 2 She has got her BA honours now. It started from day one … right through college and then university.

Interviewer So what's your son doing now?
Mother 3 He's doing computing.
Interviewer So did he go to university?
Mother 3 No. He went to college to train and is working now.

The level of educational and employment achievements of some of the children may not appear particularly outstanding or exceptional. However, if ethnic origin, and therefore vulnerability to racial discrimination, are taken into account, the people mentioned here are very successful, especially as most of them are working-class. The success of these former pupils of Marcus Garvey Nursery is even more encouraging given the research that demonstrates how black youngsters are disproportionately represented in various types of social exclusion, such as educational under-achievement, school exclusion, unemployment, imprisonment and institutional psychiatric admissions.[22, 23, 24, 25, 26, 27] How much of their success can be put down to their social, cultural and educational experiences at Marcus Garvey Nursery is difficult to ascertain and something that could be pursued in further research. What we do know, however, is that high quality early years experiences have a great impact on the life chances of children.[28, 29] Given the discrimination facing black people, the experience provided at a nursery like Marcus Garvey is perhaps even more important. The fruits of the labour at Marcus Garvey were by no means instant. The vision of Syble and the early founders was ultimately realised a quarter of a century later – as the Ackroyd workers put it: 'We didn't give up.'

Provision for parents

Earlier in this book (Chapter 2) we discussed the contribution that community nurseries make in combating social exclusion. Ethnic origin is a crucial factor in understanding social exclusion and it often impacts alongside other indicators of social exclusion. For example, some of the parents of the children at Marcus Garvey Nursery were lone mothers, some of whom helped out in the nursery in a voluntary capacity. The impact of the nursery upon these parents was remarkable, as we shall see below.

Parental support network

The nursery provides a parental support network in a friendly atmosphere. This enables parents to gain confidence and emotional stability, often providing the basis for the pursuit of education courses and eventually professional employment.

> I was young and a little bit confused … I had quite a few problems … As a teenager mother, who was trying to find my feet, it [the nursery] was very supportive for me … We could stay for as long as we wanted. Whatever issues we had, we could discuss [them]. And the staff team overall was quite supportive. It was a safety net for me as a young mother … It was also a safety net for a lot of other young mothers because there was a high rise in black teenage pregnancy at that stage, so we used to congregate at the nursery … So overall, Marcus Garvey … worked for me. Without that support, I don't know where I would have been today, but I knew that it had worked, because it helped me and enabled me to look at my role within the community, to empower me to be able to go out there and move on to other things. Within that time, I have worked within the caring field. For the past 20 odd years, both as a residential worker, as a field social worker and now as a project manager for an organisation where I oversee their childcare.
> *(Mother/worker)*

The socio-economic savings to society over 20 years, demonstrated in this one case of a transformation from social exclusion to inclusion, is in itself evidence of the nursery's significance and relevance. The role of the nursery in providing a forum to socialise with, and find support from, other parents endorses the evidence shared by parents and workers in Chapter 2 and Appendix 2. This was also appreciated by others in research:

> We had a strong parents' group. Yeah. It was lovely. I mean, when I use to go there the atmosphere was brilliant. We became friends with the parents. That really was a family thing. I would spend all day theerebecause I was welcomed. It was lovely … I always talk about the nursery. It has never left my mind.
>
> *(Mother)*

> There were families who saw it [the nursery] as a support.
>
> *(Former head)*

Ability to access employment and education

The argument mentioned in Chapter 2 that community nurseries play an important role in providing affordable and flexible childcare to enable parents to access employment and education was verified by further evidence at Marcus Garvey. A parent whose daughter is attending the nursery demonstrated this point:

> How many nurseries are there out there that you know have black children? And it's not just about the children, it's about the parents as well. I mean, myself, I've had a lot of encouragement. Where I am today, I wouldn't have been there without the nursery … So many people today knocking on the door, 'Can I have a nursery place please?' … September just gone, I started a degree. And I needed a nursery placement as well for my daughter … When I first started, I've been going round to a few nurseries and registering her with nurseries … I was waiting for someone to contact me that got the place for her. I don't know why, I just phoned up the nursery, and spoke to Collette [present head]. She said, Come along and we'll see if we can help you.'… the work provided here, it's very good. So I've had no complaint. In the private sector, it's about money in reality, it's just about money … on some days I'm at the University from quarter past nine till quarter past four and I don't get here till about five o'clock. Now the nursery's open until those times. You know, it caters for that, and at least I know my child's in a safe environment. She's not going from pillar to post, she's just here. I can pick her up, and she's happy … in terms of flexibility, next term my times [are]

> going to change but obviously I'll inform the nursery, and they
> know what's going on … so they can actively deal with it.

Although Marcus Garvey has never provided education and training for parents, it has always valued education and encourages parents to be educated. To do this, it has provided affordable and flexible childcare:

> We thought there was a need for people on income support and,
> basically, in order for them to develop themselves, they needed
> to go back into schooling … And some of them actually realised
> the importance of education.
>
> *(Assistant head)*

In addition to the encouragement by Marcus Garvey given to parents to study, some parents also acknowledge the importance of accessing education as an example to black children in the community:

> It's certainly been important [the nursery] because I am doing
> teacher training and it's important that you're a role model to the
> local children. You get the opportunity to continue with your studies.
> [The Head] said 'Come along and bring your daughter along.'
>
> *(Parent)*

Parental involvement

Marcus Garvey has not only been beneficial to parents (primarily lone mothers) in terms of accessing education and employment, it has also attempted to allow parents to get involved with the running and maintenance of the nursery. Staff saw this involvement as another method to help to build the confidence of parents; thereby helping them to return to paid employment:

> I think one of the things, our primary issue was about the
> children … but we had a lot of support from parents who would
> come in and do X, Y, Z. We did a lot of fundraising which was
> supported by the parents. They would come in and give their
> time free … To assist with the children, to listen to them reading,
> doing simple number work, building stuff. Those small things.
> And quite a few parents did that. And [I] think that actually
> helped them to move on because [I] think some of them lacked
> the confidence to actually go out in the workplace.
>
> *(Assistant head)*

Parents, too, recognised the role that the nursery played in attempting to include or involve them in its activities as a means to training and supporting, building their confidence, helping them to access employment and supporting their own children's education. A lone parent summarised this position:

> After visiting the nursery for some time, I got roped in. Started off as the cook. I couldn't cook, but on the day I was roped in, you know, 'blanch the cabbage'. How do you do that? And that sort of thing, but she [the head] was there standing there and saying, 'Well, this is how you do it.' And within a couple of weeks, I then went to work as a nursery assistant within the nursery. So, I was there to work alongside my child and the other staff. ... Anybody who comes into the nursery as a parent, you were not allowed to just leave your child and go off. It was about learning about what was actually happening. It was a learning process for the parents as well.

Serving the wider black community

Marcus Garvey not only serves the needs of pre-school black children and their parents, it also has several roles in meeting the needs of the wider community. The community and Marcus Garvey Nursery work in partnership. Here, the community's commitment to the nursery is evident:

> The staff would come to a social on Saturday night for the community. They would organise a social in here for parents.
>
> *(Former committee member)*

> Every year in October or September we used to have ... a buffet and dance – Caribbean night and it would be for the parents and the committee. Everybody mixed. And at one point, there was a lot of stray black students in Birmingham that would come here. At one point, we had that black psychologist, [name] come here.
>
> *(Former head)*

> Even [name] came through, at one period ... Oh, what's the name of that poet from London? He would come through and do stuff. [name]
>
> *(Former committee member)*

Surprisingly, given the nursery's focus on serving the black community, the community idea did not just extend to black people but meant all the local residents. Syble Morgan points out:

> It [the nursery] was born out of a community organisation so whatever we did was community-oriented. Like at Christmas time, I used to have two parties. There was one Christmas party for the children who came here. There was one Christmas community party. There is a school down there and there is a school across there and I would go there and ask the school to send children to this [community] party that wouldn't go to a party normally and therefore we would always have a full party.

At other times in the nursery's history, it was essentially the black community that serviced the nursery. It was apparent that social engagement and involvement in community affairs would strengthen the links in the neighbourhood:

> **Former head** Auntie Ivy, that was the cleaner then, her husband used to do a lot of the repair work here for half price or for nothing, and there were people in the community who saw that it was a good thing for the community, not just for us …
> **Parent** People who were skilled.
> **Former head** Yes … they give it for free. Before I start up here, I go round and beg chairs and tables and from schools that was closing down and whatever. And the few people who lived at my house with me would come back with me [to the nursery] half past six, seven o'clock at night, and paint the chairs and tables and they weren't working [at the nursery]. They had their own job. But they believed in what we were trying to do and on a whole we had a lot of the community with us.

Although the history of the nursery was premised upon a significant responsibility to the black community and vice versa, like many other community activities in the 1980s, this dwindled substantially, although not entirely. Now, the nursery is seen as mainly an early years provider rather than a community project, according to the present head:

> That's what we need to go back to … It not the lack of determination or not wanting it to be done. It is more seen now as a nursery project rather than a community project. We don't see the community, like, well I haven't.

Active community participation in the life of the nursery is now seen only through involvement of volunteers in day-to-day childcare and play. Two volunteers portray their contribution to the nursery:

> I was coming here just to visit Tammy [his girlfriend and careworker] on her lunch break and then … I don't know, the kids just sort of adapted to me … One time I was leaving and Collette asked me if I wanted to come back on a voluntary basis. And I said, 'Yeah, I didn't mind', because I was getting on with the kids and getting on with everyone else that was working here … I thought I might as well come in and get some experience … because it is Marcus Garvey Nursery … because I live in this area anyway. So I feel like I'm doing something for the community, for the black community.
>
> *(Volunteer)*

> I am always here, because I live in the area. In my spare time, I volunteer my time, like, looking after the kids and whatever, like I will be standing in and I'll help them, and you know what I mean? Look after the kids … I'm a male figure round them … there's nuff[30] females and sometimes the kids like to see men. I work in the community, mental health work …
>
> *(Community worker)*

Whether the present head captures the community idea or not, current plans to introduce neighbourhood nurseries are forcing her, along with the Harambee management, to rethink how best to maximise the use of the nursery. Plans to extend the building and expand the services to incorporate and serve the wider community are presently underway. Marcus Garvey still has the potential to provide a service to the black community. This does not mean a return to the nursery's past or a replication of services other than childcare and early years education. What is needed is an examination of the ideas and practices that embrace the notion of community in the twenty-first century. Only time will tell what can be accomplished in the coming years.

Concluding discussion: implications for 'community nursery' provision

The role that Marcus Garvey continues to play is essential in providing services to pre-school black children, their parents and the wider black community. No other nursery in the area has Marcus Garvey's focus, which is almost exclusively on serving African-Caribbean people.

For the children, early years education and childcare is provided in which a sense of culture and identity is absorbed through a focus on black culture. The needs of parents are served by the nursery providing affordable and flexible childcare, social support and involvement in activities in a homely environment and also the encouragement for parents to access education and employment. The nursery has traditionally sought to cater for the wider community through providing social activities. It continues to do this but plans to revive the more extensive community engagement, as witnessed in its past, as part of its expansion of services. In spite of all this provision, Marcus Garvey operates under extreme funding constraints and is vulnerable to racial discrimination. That, however, does not mean the need for Marcus Garvey's services is any less. This is neatly summarised by one of the original workers:

> We have not alleviated this issue of black children under-achieving ... I feel the need is still there for that kind of input [referring to the nursery]. Because with each generation, even the children that we taught ... and I am not excusing parents because they should make the time to teach the children about history and culture and the 3Rs, but I think to get it in a structured way on a day-to-day basis ... Marcus Garvey still serves that purpose. I know that there have been rumblings over the last couple of years about actually closing it because of the lack of funding. But I think no matter how hard people try, they can't detract from the fact that there is a need. That need is still there. I mean, it may seem that there is more access for black people but there is an underlying factor that I feel that needs to be addressed by black people for black people and that Marcus Garvey serves that purpose.

While acknowledging that the needs of black children have not diminished, there was a feeling that nurseries like Marcus Garvey, by providing for the black children, actually discouraged mainstream provision from developing their services also to cater for the black community. The assistant head noted:

> But, I think, small pockets of people doing small things like the
> Marcus Garvey Nursery is like pouring water into a bucket full of
> water, it gets nowhere or it gets dispersed so quickly that you
> can't see it. What we do need is something that says success is
> around and can be made. And it shouldn't be left isolated to the
> black community to cater for the whole of the black community
> because this is the thing about the black looking after their own
> which has been bandied around for so many years that prevents
> the mainstream from developing their services for black people.
> If black people take care of their own, they [the mainstream]
> don't have to provide anything.

However, this view was not unanimous. One father was totally opposed to integrating
black services in the manner suggested by the assistant head. He was especially
concerned about reliance on support from outside the black community:

> Basically you wouldn't get a chef to fix a car, so I wouldn't have
> the local authority to interfere in something that they have no
> business or no knowledge of … you know, if you let a chef lose
> on your car, your car ain't going to drive … I think, really and
> truly, it's time we realise we have to fund our own salvation, our
> own liberation. So the people need to fund it, not the state. I
> agree, the state is the people but the state just want our tax
> money but … I've never seen my income tax … it's always been
> taken, so what I don't see, I don't miss. So let them keep it, and
> the little money I've got, I don't mind giving it to support this as
> long as my brother and sister supports it too. If we all give a
> pound a week, you know, something like this could be bigger …
> And that's what's more critical, self-reliance … support, buying in
> what we believe in and what we need than running to the man
> who doesn't care, doesn't know. So, you know, I think it's better
> we try and support ourselves.

Whether Marcus Garvey should be integrated with other services or not is something
that is likely to fuel debate amongst staff and parents well into the future. What is
not debatable is the fact that Marcus Garvey is an important resource for the black
community in Handsworth and that more of such provision is needed.

7 The end or just the beginning? Community nurseries in neighbourhoods

In this book we have discussed the history of, and prospects for, community nurseries. We examined the underpinning concept of community and what that meant to the nurseries included as case studies. The category 'community nursery' is not widely understood. Such nurseries are often regarded as yet another form of childcare provision, and their role in community support and involvement has been largely ignored. This has partly been because community nurseries have often developed as self-help initiatives outside of conventional professional interventions.

The 250 or so community nurseries mostly belong to the non-profit, voluntary sector and were set up primarily, but not exclusively, to cater for the needs of working parents who could not afford more expensive private care for their children. They also saw themselves as having a role in their local community by offering various kinds of support to young families and others in the community. But community nurseries do not have to belong to the voluntary sector. Robert Owen Early Years Centre illustrates the potential for hybrid arrangements with the state sector. In Chapter 5 Judy Stephenson (the Head of Robert Owen Early Years Centre) argues that the state education sector can, and should, become much more responsive to the local community and be able to offer not only childcare but also other community-oriented services. Many nursery school head teachers share her views.[1]

Sustainability - The Critical Issue

These different kinds of community nurseries have in common a commitment to providing affordable all-day childcare and serving their local community (however defined) in other ways. They do not view the services they provide as a profit-making business. Given their location, almost always in poor or mixed communities, they have very great difficulty meeting all their costs from the fees they charge. On average, the fees charged for a childcare place from £134 per week per child in

London to £88 per week per child in the north-east.[2] These fees cover staff costs and other expenses. All childcare providers are required to meet regulatory standards in terms of staffing, and make sure that staff-child ratios, set by legislation, are upheld. In particular, they must provide one to three ratios for babies and maintain that ratio all the time they are open. Babycare is therefore very expensive even if staff receive low wages. This means that few economies can be made in the numbers of staff employed.

Many parents cannot afford to pay the fees that would cover staff wages in a nursery. Low-income parents may claim childcare allowances, but since such claims are made through employers, parents must first of all have the kind of regular employment whereby the employer co-operates with the claim to childcare allowance. Many twilight jobs in the informal (or black market) sector such as bar-work (offering cash-in-hand without benefits) cannot be used to claim childcare allowances. And as Chapter 2 illustrates, the operation of the tax and benefit schemes are complex and routes into work, particularly for women who are under-qualified and have been out of work for a long time, are very problematic.[3]

In any event, the subsidies do not meet the entire cost of childcare; parents must make up the difference. Community nurseries may recoup some money by charging scaled fees, that is, richer parents subsidising poorer ones. But given that community nurseries serve mostly low-income or mixed communities, they must rely on grants and fundraising to meet the shortfall in fees. The cost of providing flexible childcare and other forms of support *cannot* be met entirely from fees paid by parents in poor communities. Almost all community nurseries receive some kind of subsidy from their local authority or some other agency. They illustrate the failure of the market to provide childcare for children from poor communities. Community nurseries therefore fill a gap in the childcare market but they survive only precariously. Could they do better? Where do they fit into the wider picture of early years education and care? How could policy initiatives capitalise on what they have to offer? In order to address this question, we have to look at the spectrum of initiatives which have characterised this government's policies on early education and care.

Contradictory initiatives
The National Childcare Strategy

The government has always held the view that parents should be responsible for locating and paying for their own childcare. The National Childcare Strategy does not challenge this view of a market place in childcare for working parents, but instead seeks to manipulate the market by offering more financial incentives to working parents seeking childcare. Since the National Childcare Strategy has been introduced, there has been a huge growth in the private sector in response to the strategy's emphasis on working mothers. There are now more than 20 commercial nursery chains, attracting big investors.[4] The Working Families' Tax Credit and other tax and benefit breaks enable parents to buy in childcare, although it is still expensive. Some of these tax and benefit breaks have been used by parents to buy places at community nurseries, but as pointed out in Chapter 2, assumptions about the availability of tax and benefit breaks have led some local authorities to reduce their grants to community nurseries.

The National Childcare Strategy has also made funds available for entrepreneurs, both in the private sector and in the voluntary sector, to claim extra one-off monies for particular projects. These monies are mainly administered through EYDCPs (see pp. 73-5). There are at least 55 of these funding streams, all with their own time-scales and criteria, and all of them short-term and mostly for capital expenditure rather than for revenue. This 'lollipop' approach, as opposed to systematic, planned and regular funding, has been much criticised.[5] Some community nurseries have undoubtedly benefited from these initiatives in the short term, but in the long term they do not change the prospects for sustainability and long-term viability.

Nursery education

Recent education policies have confirmed the right of children to access state-funded nursery education services, but only for a short period in the day. The nursery education entitlement most often takes place in a primary or nursery school with more highly qualified and better remunerated staff, namely teachers working at nationally agreed rates of pay. Children also start school in the year in which they are four, the earliest school age in Europe.[6] These nursery education and schooling entitlements have been created independently of, and without reference to, the National Childcare Strategy and stem from a concern with educational standards of numeracy and literacy.

The Government has provided a standard funding allowance for nursery education for all four-year-olds and for 80 per cent of three-year-olds. The funding allowance for four-year-olds has mostly been allocated to maintained schools, who admit children either to nursery or reception classes or to some hybrid of the two. If no school-based nursery classes are available, the funds can be given to private and voluntary sector providers. Unlike schools, they do not have to employ qualified teachers in order to offer nursery education.[7] The nursery education funds for three-year-olds are intended *mainly* for the private and voluntary sector. It has been left up to EYDCPs to allocate and administer the funds for both three- and four-year-olds.

All four-year-olds and 80 per cent of three-year-olds are now entitled to nursery education since September 1998 under the Nursery Education and Grant Maintained Schools Act 1996. However, this nursery education, at least for most four-year-olds, now takes place in schools. Children of working parents, who need childcare as well as education, require additional arrangements. The current term now being used to describe childcare for those children who attend school premises for their nursery education entitlement is 'wrap-around care'. Unless the school offers childcare, it usually means that children spend part of the day in one place and the rest of it in another place. Even where the school offers childcare, it usually has to be offered under different rules and regulations and with different staffing arrangements. Children, for example, may be able to access parts of the nursery school, such as the garden or kitchen, whilst they are receiving 'nursery education' but not for the rest of the day when they receive 'wrap-around care'. In this way, administrative categories work against the best interests of the children. Robert Owen, by taking a deliberately community-based approach has managed to avoid this pitfall, but most school-based childcare does not.[8]

This nursery education entitlement leaves community nurseries in a difficult position. From once having been able to offer full-time continuous care, community nurseries must now either qualify as nursery education providers (as Ackroyd has reluctantly done), or lose their three- and four-year-old children for at least part of the day to a neighbouring school and arrange to have them delivered and collected as High Peak does. On the other hand, if they do offer nursery education, they are financially undercutting schools because they can offer nursery education without qualified teachers and without the equipment and space that many schools can offer. As a result, many nursery schools feel threatened by private and voluntary nursery provision which claims to offer nursery education but without qualified teachers and a high standard of facilities.[9] On the other hand, non-maintained education provision, including community nurseries, often claim to be providing a 'good education' by virtue of a Section 122 Ofsted inspection, which does not require teachers to deliver the curriculum, and which is far less rigorous in its scope and in terms of the standards of provision it requires, than the inspections of maintained education provision (see note 7). This is a divisive situation which can only be resolved through more coherent policy making.

Sure Start

Sure Start is yet another separate government initiative. It is specifically aimed at children aged under three in targeted poor communities. The Government aims to have 500 Sure Start programmes in place by 2006 – the end of its second term of office. The rhetoric that governed the National Childcare Strategy and the introduction of tax and benefit reforms, ignored the lack of confidence experienced by poor women in poor communities and assumed the transition to work would be relatively straightforward. The Sure Start programme, by contrast, is a preventive measure that focuses specifically on family support for mothers and children. The Treasury has set Sure Start a number of specific targets such as better birth-weights and health in young children; improved educational performance when children reach school; and fewer speech and behavioural problems. Increased employment for mothers is not amongst these targets, since the emphasis of this initiative is on improving the life-chances of very young children in poor communities, in the hope of tackling poverty in the longterm. [10]

Sure Start has an explicit community development rhetoric and the emphasis of the programmes is on 'joined-up thinking' amongst the professionals delivering the services. The intention is that a cross sector of local professionals from education, health and social work will work with local women to devise a range of family support programmes and facilities in the targeted neighbourhoods. The family support offered by Sure Start may or may not include childcare. A £20 million, five-year monitoring programme for Sure Start underpins the programme. This prestigious programme has so far ignored community nurseries as a phenomenon worth taking into account, possibly because community nurseries still exist largely outside conventional professional orbits.

Centres of Early Excellence

Yet another competing initiative, this time an educational one, impinges on community nurseries. Centres of Early Excellence are mostly education-based centres which claim to offer a wide range of facilities, including nursery education, daycare and a range of facilities for local parents. The intention is to increase the number of these Centres of Early Excellence to 100 by 2005. These centres are highly professionalised and well-funded, attracting additional monies from the DfES. This is sometimes resented by neighbouring early years facilities who have to get by on much less money.[11] Centres of Early Excellence also still experience problems in reconciling the different philosophies and practices governing education and childcare. One of the most persistent of these problems is the question of the terms and conditions of the staff employed. Teachers and nursery nurses are differently qualified and remunerated. This has led to many of the centres being run as parallel care and education establishments on the same premises. Very few centres have fully integrated staffing.[12]

Whilst most community nurseries cannot afford to employ teachers, on the other hand, their staffing policies have usually emphasised the importance of local recruitment and collective decision-making. Ackroyd has a policy of only employing local people, and has had a remarkable continuity of staff. Marcus Garvey employs black people to reflect the needs of the black community served by the nursery. Robert Owen also employs local, unqualified women who are being enabled to work towards NVQs.

Childminding networks

Registered childminders have traditionally provided most childcare places in poor communities. For some parents, childminders are a positive choice because they are home-based in an individualised domestic setting, which for very young children is sometimes regarded as preferable. However, turnover is high and in some cases external controls and supervision are limited to registration and inspection visits. If the childminder lives in a poor community, for example in a high-rise block, it is likely that she (98 per cent of registered childminders are women) will only be able to offer a similarly restricted physical environment to the one the children in her care come from. In such circumstances, for example, children will have access to outside play and learning only if childminders choose to take the children out to playgrounds and parks and other groups where early years children are supported, entertained and catered for. In addition, the number of childminders fluctuates with the labour market and when employment opportunities for women are good, as at present, then recruitment and retention of childminders is more difficult.

The Government has attempted to recruit more childminders and supported the development of childminding networks, so that a nominated group of childminders can be provided with regular advice, support and training and a place to meet. Many registered childminders study for the Certificate in Childminding Practice (CCP) and/or link with NVQ qualifications. Registered childminders are supported within the network and/or by local authority registration officers, although this situation will change as local authority inspection and registration functions are being transferred to Ofsted. Ackroyd and Robert Owen have both supported childminders in this way, the former informally and the latter formally. But childminder numbers have recently fallen dramatically. The predictions are that with the transfer of local registration officers to Ofsted, many more childminders will give up rather than face the formalities of Ofsted inspections.[13]

Childminders offer a relatively inexpensive solution (to government if not to parents) for increasing the number of childcare places. But even where networks have been set up, anecdotal evidence suggests that unregistered childminding (which is illegal and therefore not the same as registered childminding) continues to operate because for some parents it is the only affordable/available choice to them.

Neighbourhood Nurseries

Despite the above initiatives, the Government continues to experience problems in the take-up of benefits and equality of access to services amid the growing social exclusion and deepening poverty in disaffected communities. For various reasons, to do with political credibility and priorities, together with the constraints of departmental thinking within the DfES, this wider picture of inequality has not been adequately addressed. Instead each initiative is viewed in its own narrow terms as a success, in that some limited improvement has been achieved. But these initiatives are not seen as related to one another and their inherent contradictions and limitations have not been addressed in policy terms. There has been very little discussion about contradictions or priorities between existing provisions, or how these various forms of provision can be developed or expanded, and what kind of legislation or funding patterns would best support them.

In response to campaigning about the lack of affordable childcare in poor communities, the Government has launched yet another new initiative, Neighbourhood Nurseries, as part of the National Childcare Strategy in 2000.[14] A glossy leaflet proclaims that it will provide 'a nursery in every neighbourhood'. The intention is to create an additional 45,000 new childcare places, that is, the equivalent of 900 new 50-place nurseries. Delivery is to be achieved quickly by taking £203 million capital from the DfES and a further £100 million capital from the New Opportunities Fund. Each new nursery may claim up to three years' funding; that is, up to £150,000 the first year, £90,000 the second and £30,000 the third. Since this capital and revenue is nowhere near enough to fund 900 new nurseries, or guarantee their continuity after three years, the government is seeking a range of partners 'from nursery providers to banks, community organisations and, in some cases, employers' to turn the vision into reality. Each existing provider is to be asked to create new places for children in poor communities, even if the provision lies outside the community itself. There is nothing in the leaflet to suggest the neighbourhood nurseries might have any other function besides providing childcare places. At the time of writing the DfES has issued a tender document for the provision of training to the 900 nursery managers whose nurseries, it is assumed, will provide the requisite number of neighbourhood nursery places. This training is for delivering adult literacy skills to the poor and semi-literate mothers whose children are projected to take up the neighbourhood nursery places. The assumption, in the tender document, is that the provision of such skills within the nursery will enable newly competent mothers to seek employment, and therefore become better able to meet the costs of the nursery. There is no mention of the 250 community nurseries or the 500 nursery schools which could have been used strategically to support such a neighbourhood nursery initiative, although ironically, Robert Owen Nursery Centre, which was up and running after *years* of effort, is cited as one of three examples of a neighbourhood nursery.

The Neighbourhood Nurseries initiative illustrates that a continued belief in the local marketplace still underpins the National Childcare Strategy. The assumption remains unchallenged that with a little pump priming, the market, in all its diversity, can be manipulated to meet government targets for childcare places. The state can call on others to supplement the costs, even for the poorest children. Since this 'partnership' is so important, it would be unwise to favour one form of provision over another, or to exclude any provider from the initiative.

The agency which is responsible for administering the policy at a local level is the EYDCP. We consider next the effectiveness of EYDCPs in providing local coordination and support, and trying to meet Government targets in early years.

Early Years Development and Childcare Partnership (EYDCPs)

Functions

Government policy has promoted the growth of partnerships in many areas, supplementing or replacing the planning, financing and implementation of publicly-run services with a mixed economy of private and voluntary input. EYDCPs are an example of this wider shift of policy.[15] EYDCPs were first set up by statute in 1997.

Each local authority is required to set up an early years partnership. Originally their remit was to oversee the fair allocation of nursery places, in the wake of the voucher scheme, but, as outlined below, this remit has been considerably expanded.

EYDCPs are serviced by a lead officer appointed by the local authority. They are chaired (hopefully) by a representative of the local community. Membership of partnerships is voluntary and is intended to reflect the range of early education and child interests within the authority, including those of parents.

EYDCPs have grown considerably in their range and function since their inception. They now act as the planning vehicle for a range of early education and childcare developments. They handle considerable budgets and access many of the special funds set up to generate more childcare. They now, through the local authority, employ a range of staff, including staff to oversee business development. The local authority, on behalf of the partnership, is required to submit regular plans and accounts to DfES.

Development of EYDCPs has to an extent been for a particular purpose only, as new functions have been added to their remit by central government. The 150 EYDCPs are now serviced by a team of 18 advisers based at the DfES and supported by a series of regional and national meetings, and by a series of publications giving advice on various aspects of their functioning.

The remit of the EYDCPs is now described as:

- To identify and map childcare provision and needs amongst all groups within the local area.
- To work collaboratively with voluntary, community and private providers to increase availability and accessibility of provision.
- To ensure quality of provision.
- To ensure provision is affordable for groups who might otherwise be excluded.
- To ensure good and accessible information on services that are available.

EYDCPs were set up by statute and the ultimate responsibility lies with the local authority. Membership of EYDCPs is voluntary, and members have been asked, or volunteered, to take part on the basis that they 'represent' certain interests. Members are entitled to sit on the partnership board, are eligible to serve on its subcommittees and they receive information concerning the partnership. But members are not usually representatives in a formal elected sense. In many cases it would be hard to define the group who is being represented by a particular member, or who constitutes the wider pool of people from whom membership selection is being made. In addition, many members are inactive. Often the interests of members are in conflict. If money is limited, as it almost always is, decisions have to be made. Aid granted to one group can only be made at the expense of another. How can such choices can be made fairly if the members making the decisions are also those who stand to gain by them?

The focus of decision-making has therefore been somewhat uncertain, both within EYDCPs and in relation to the local authority of which they are a part. If there is any kind of dispute and the members of the EYDCP challenge the agendas, plans or data compiled by the authority, the local authority is in difficulty. Uncertainty about membership, its representation and requirements, and members' status and rights is a constant theme within EYDCPs. So, in turn, is their uncertainty about the status of the EYDCP within the spectrum of local authority work. On what issues should they be consulted? Where do they stand in relation to social services, health or education provision? How much should they try to cooperate or intervene in other issues they consider to be relevant? Where do the boundaries of their work lie?

In order to make sure government aims are met, and EYDCPs are held fully accountable for their delivery, the DfES has issued a series of directives and timetables for submission of information and bids for money. The degree of centralised involvement inevitably conflicts with the wish to encourage local autonomy and decision making, an issue that has also dogged the Sure Start programme[16]. The level of demands and the pace of change demanded by the DfES has been seen by many of the officers and members of EYDCPs as distorting the agendas of partnerships and counterproductive to the growth of local responsiveness and discussion.

Whatever their shortcomings, and in the absence of any other vehicle, the Government continues to use EYDCPs as an instrument for delivering early years policy. EYDCPs must now appoint business or finance managers to assist providers to apply for the monies and budget to increase their number of childcare places to meet Government targets, especially the targets for Neighbourhood Nurseries.

Support and development work

Before EYDCPs were set up in 1997, support and development work for voluntary and private sector childcare provision was mostly located in social services departments, although in a few local authorities, mainly in London, all social service functions for early years provision were transferred to education departments. Social services departments were also responsible for registration and inspection of voluntary and private sector childcare.

These social services functions have now mostly been eroded. Responsibility for registration and inspection, which often used to include advice and support for new and existing providers, as from September 2001, has been transferred to Ofsted. EYDCPs are now in the process of taking over the remaining social services advisory and development posts, either as part of, or in close conjunction with, business managers and advisers.

In a few instances, there have been local support networks for community nurseries. In some cities support networks for community nurseries have been set up. The Sheffield Community Childcare Network has for some time provided a forum for the community nurseries within the city. In Birmingham the EYDCP, along with the Birmingham Voluntary Sector Council has, since 2000, put forward a project (namely the Quality Childcare Support Services) specifically to offer support for the voluntary childcare sector. This is in addition to Small Steps, which was set up in Birmingham in 1994 as a support network for community nursery managers. Marcus Garvey Nursery is actively involved in Small Steps. Robert Owen works very closely with the EYDCP, which holds many of its activities at the nursery. Such support increasingly depends on the identification by the EYDCP of the category of community nurseries and their understanding of the contribution that they can make.

However, most community nurseries appear to be regarded within EYDCPs not as evidence of a special sector warranting specific support but as just one provider of childcare amongst many. As a provider, they may benefit from specific small grants administered by the EYDCP for outside space, IT equipment or staff training, for example. Community nurseries have not been seen as representatives of a distinct movement or a sector with recognisable objectives and procedures, whose interests should be supported and promoted. This book suggests that, in fact, they may have a useful role to play.

A role for community nurseries under New Labour's childcare and early education policies?

The social, political and economic climate has undoubtedly changed over the last two decades. The traditional, communitarian ethos that characterise community nurseries like Ackroyd and Marcus Garvey Nurseries has largely disappeared. Service provision is more market-led and market-driven. For the market is about profits and competition and relies on a view of parents as consumers exercising individual choices, choices that depend invariably on income and mobility. The paradox is that community nurseries have traditionally catered for the needs of deprived communities who lack the income and mobility to exercise market choice, yet under present government policy initiatives and intentions, not only are they being ignored, but they are endangered. Does this matter if places are being provided elsewhere?

Based on the case studies we have used in this book, we argue that community nurseries do still have an important role to play. They illustrate issues about the shortcomings of the marketplace in childcare, and the problems of reconciling care and education, in particular, over definitions of what constitutes early education and who should deliver it.

They also raise important questions about community development and social exclusion. Who is the community being served? Can or should a nursery be a focal point of the community? What is the role of professionals who do not live in or are not part of that community? Who defines the community and what if it is not geographical but, like Marcus Garvey, based on notions of ethnicity? Our argument is that community nurseries do provide useful and diverse models for future developments in childcare and education.

The clock cannot be turned back and some of the original community nurseries, such as 123, would find themselves out of kilter in today's world. But many of the principles on which the community nurseries were founded are still relevant and seem to characterise some of the principles of the new Neigbourhoud Nursery Initiative and other current policy provision in early years. Most provision, we argue, should and could meet the following principles which have been restated in many forms and in many places.[17, 18, 19]

Cohesive – care and education are historical, administrative divisions which are meaningless, and sometimes harmful to children themselves; childcare and education should be continuous and provided in the same place at the same time, meeting both parents' needs for flexibility *and* children's needs for continuity.
Comprehensive – a broad curriculum framework offering children opportunities to learn, play, rest, eat, run and jump, dance, sing, etc. for *all* children in the area, irrespective of race or disability.
On the doorstep – a place in the neighbourhood set aside for a nursery and community meeting place.
Locally managed – staff and parents work together to set and implement their own policies.
Local workers – the nursery is staffed, or partly staffed, by people from the same community that is being served, with opportunities for continuous training.

Catchment based – catchment (however the community catchment is defined), rather than income, determines access.

Affordable – an acceptance that nurseries in poor areas will be partly or mainly dependent on public grants and funding to achieve the highest standards.

Children as part of the community – children, like adults, have wit, imagination, originality and the capacity to care. Children should not be shut away in a totally safe and sterile environment with a cohort of other children nearly or exactly the same age. Children enjoy and learn from everyday activities in inter-generational surroundings.

Supportive – a recognition of the inter-dependency of work and family life for mothers and fathers, and the tensions of reconciling them; and sympathetic understanding of the variations in health and family circumstances that most families experience.

Diversity – understanding and addressing issues of ethnic and religious differences, particularly for those at the margins of society.

This is not an unobtainable paradise but everyday reality for some children in some countries. Indeed, as we have shown, most of the government initiatives in England *already* support one or another of these principles: an entitlement for all children, flexible childcare, neighbourhood support, a good curricular framework, local coordination. But they do not add up to a coherent policy. Different aspects of provision work against one another and the contradictions between different policies and different kinds of provision have never been addressed. The issue is not the narrower goal of supporting community nurseries come what may, but the wider goal of developing a coherent and integrated policy, where provision consists of a partnership between the differing sectors for the good of each sector independently and all sectors as a collective group,[20] for early years education and care. Sally Holterman, recently writing for Daycare Trust[21], has suggested one such blueprint for developing a coherent neighbourhood-based policy that incorporates community nurseries. Others have also been suggested. [22]

Community nurseries are non-profit, locally managed, flexible childcare services operating in poor neighbourhoods, which are particularly alert to the needs of the communities they serve, however defined. The Government needs to address the nuances and divisions of the early education and care provision that have been created. Reconsidering the Neighbourhood Nurseries initiative and the role played by existing community nurseries would show, after many omissions, that joined-up thinking, in early education and care, is still possible.

Appendix 1
The nurseries in the survey

The Barn

The Barn is in London. It aims to offer half of its places to working parents and half to parents who are in education or who are not working. The nursery receives substantial funding from its local authority. In return, the local authority takes an active role in setting fee levels and financial targets for the nursery.

The Big Wheel

The Big Wheel is in a seaside town on the East Coast of England. The town has the most deprived areas of the county it is in. The nursery is part of a small charity whose main concern is to help teenage mothers. In addition to offering full daycare, the nursery is also part of an education and housing project for young parents.

The Bridge

The Bridge is on the fringes of a new town in the West Midlands. It started as a playgroup 30 years ago and developed full daycare facilities in order to survive when it took over the lease of the building in which it is located. In addition to full daycare, the nursery has a thriving pre-school service.

The Castle

The Castle is located in a small town in rural West Midlands. The nursery has a close relationship – probably due to its former life as a local authority nursery – with social services and is a main provider of childcare for children 'in need' in the area.

The Cathedral

The Cathedral is in London and started as a playgroup. The nursery takes full time children only and charges all parents – whatever their income – the same amount, apart from those children who are 'in need' and are therefore funded by social services.

High Peaks

High Peaks is in the second most deprived ward of a small East Midlands city, a ward that has high rates of unemployment, lone mothers and social rented housing. The nursery has a training room that is well stocked with computer equipment and runs courses aimed at increasing the confidence, assertiveness and job readiness of mainly lone mothers living in the locality. The European Social Fund and a local college fund the training aspect of the nursery's work.

The Tree House

The Tree House is in a large East Midlands city. The area in which it is located, as the manager said, is 'one of the poorest' of the city. It has high rates of unemployment and lone motherhood. The nursery has a training room, developed to attract further funding from the local authority, in which mainly childcare and computing courses are run.

The Walk

The Walk nursery is in London. The nursery has a mix of parents. It has full fee-payers, parents whose children are 'in need' and who are therefore funded by the local authority, and a number of women who are at college through a 'women in the workplace' initiative.

White Horses

White Horses is located in a small rural town in the south-east. Of all the community nurseries where interviews were carried out after conducting the survey investigation, White Horses had the most affluent parents, some of whom spoke of their own and their partner's employment in London. The nursery has close links with the community secondary school in the town.

Appendix 2
Experiences from the chalkface: Stories from parents and workers

These stories aim to supplement the data of parents and workers already mentioned in this book. They were given by two parents and two careworkers at a recent community nurseries workshop.[1] The stories are accounts of events as the parents and workers perceive them. By presenting the direct account of people involved in community nurseries we intend to give the participants a 'voice'. It is the release of participants' voices that make these statements particularly powerful. The voices of participants are also heard in other early years books.[2, 3, 4] However, in the community nurseries workshop, the proceedings on which this book is based, parents and workers were given a free reign to air their opinions. In their presentations to the workshop parents and workers were neither prompted, probed nor interrupted as they would be in interviews or group discussions. The aim was to listen to the experiences of parents and workers without their experiences being analysed and interpreted by third parties. We start with the accounts of the parents followed by the workers.

Parent of Jenny, who attends Foundations Day Nursery, Birmingham

The day arrived when after the birth of my daughter I had to return to work and arrange childcare. So by word of mouth and thumbing through the trusty Yellow Pages, I had a list of phone numbers and a home-made questionnaire that these nurseries would have to pass before they would even get within sniffing distance of my precious bundle. Several of the nurseries fell on the first hurdle – a hurried remark, the inability to answer a direct question, little or no flexibility with changing days or just a disinterested tone, all resulted with the nursery in question being scored off my list of possibilities. If they couldn't be bothered to take an interest in me, a prospective customer, what chance did my poor little angel have once removed from my never blinking mother's gaze? My ever-shrinking shortlist of possibilities was narrowed down to a list of appointments where I could view the prospective nursery that may be lucky enough to care for my child. I was invited to spend an afternoon with my daughter at Foundations. I took her along not quite knowing what to expect. I knew what I didn't want, that is, a cold environment where children were seen as a number. The thought of my baby being scared or unhappy is just unbearable. In the Pooh Bear room I saw children toddling around, colourful toys within easy access and being played with in a relaxed environment and small children climbing over and hugging a nursery nurse as she told me about daily activities. I watched how the children interacted with the staff and each other. What really sold it for me was, as I was leaving. I saw a small girl about to leave with her mother. Before she did so, she turned to her nursery nurse, with outstretched arms, and planted a sloppy wet kiss on her cheek.

My initial feeling towards Foundations has proved right. My daughter has been there for about 18 months. She is extremely bright. This is nurtured in a non-pressurised way. She enjoys her days and looks forward to going. My daughter is not yet three-years-old. She knows her way around a computer, her colours and more songs than I could teach her. Well done Marie and all the staff for taking such good care of Jenny. Her baby sister will be with you come October.

Sue Downing, parent and community manager

I wonder if you would all help me? Could you give me a rendition of 'Miss Polly had a dolly':

> Miss Polly had a dolly who was sick, sick, sick
> So she called for the doctor to come quick, quick, quick.
> The doctor came with his bag and his hat
> And he knocked on the door with a rat-a-tat-tat.
> He looked at the dolly and he shook his head,
> He said 'Miss Polly, put her straight to bed',
> He wrote on the paper for a pill, pill, pill,
> 'I'll be back in the morning with the bill, bill, bill.'

That was the first thing I learned as a young mum, going along when my child started playgroup. I lived on a housing estate [with] a thousand cheaply built houses for the working class families on the borders of Birmingham and Great Barr ... Like many of those developments in the sixties and seventies, not very much attention was given to community provision. And Walsall Council met together with a group of mums and this was the start, really, of the playgroup movement. And they erected a big building on the edge of the estate and then charged a peppercorn rent of a pound a year for the mums to lease the building and in that building they ran 10 sessions a week, a playgroup for those people in the area … The sessions were supervised by the mums in that community. Every mum that walked through the door was encouraged to be on the rota to go and help and do mundane things as mixing the drinks, making the coffee for the staff, washing the paint pots, all sorts of things that make this kind of play environment run smoothly. And when Max started the playgroup, I walked in and some lovely warmth enveloped me. It was really, really good.

I got married at 19. Max was born at 21. I'd worked as an office junior here, and an office junior there, all sort of menial tasks within the office system. And I didn't really have … very high self-esteem, so just going in as an ordinary mum and being encouraged to do things that I could do was good for me. It was a big learning curve. And I can remember, I went on my first mum's help and they sang that song, and I remember singing it to myself all the way and I would not forget it, so I could do it with Max at later dates. And they did very small, very mundane, ordinary things, but it was that initial encouragement when I went into that situation, which was a big learning curve for me. All mums were encouraged to go on the committee of the school … And if you could make a commitment to attending the meetings regularly, you were welcomed on to that committee. And from that group of people, the chair, vice-chair, secretary, treasurer, there was a newsletter editor and there was a social secretary. The social secretary was the chief person. We all enjoyed ourselves in the bars, and went out and bought the Christmas presents for the children, all of those kind of nice things. And I can remember the first thing I did. I volunteered to be the leader.

That was the first of many roles throughout the next 18 years of doing that task, but this was my first experience of it. And that was really good and I had an old manual typewriter at the end of my kitchen, and I had a gestetner. Any body else remember a gestetner? What is a gestetner of all things? It was an inked duplicator that you wound the handle round and it printed off the table, like photocopying. But then I had this old gestetner in my kitchen, and I used to run off all these things. And all of this was really, really good and I felt glad my children went through the process. I mean they started in playgroup … then they went to pre-school nursery, and then they went into school. And I think that there's a sadness in that because then, you know, my children had the best, really, of that. I've seen lots of things evolved. I'm still involved with children, although not pre-school children, on a daily basis. My own children are both parents, which makes me a grandma now. My son is a very practical person. He's now got a very responsible job as a maintenance manager … My daughter is a mum … She's enjoying a few years out with her daughter while she grows up, because she enjoyed the fact that we had that privilege together and the bonding formed then. But it is an encouragement and I'm glad I've had the opportunity to share … to encourage the mums that walk in through the door, who are shy and low in self-esteem and parenting skills, still today have very, very little value in society. Probably even less now than when I was a young mum, because now you're rushed back into the work scenario again, as soon as you've almost given birth. So if you do come into contact with the mums, give them that sense of value and sense of worth and a pat on the back for bringing up the next generation.

Caroline Patrick, Childcare Manager, Austin Road Day Nursery, Birmingham

Over the last seven years I have worked in two community nurseries. For the first five years as a nursery nurse, and for the last two years, as a manager. In my experience, there are many benefits working for a community day nursery: ongoing training for staff and progression for staff within the workforce, etc. Parents and carers not only benefit from the reasonable childcare fees, but they have the opportunity to become actively involved in the running of the nursery, that is, fundraising, staffing pursuits, finances and trips, etc. The benefits above can only be achieved through a dedicated management committee.

Parents and carers work long hours which make them less likely to become active in the nursery. In the past, daycare officers would attend meetings to give advice on childcare issues. In my opinion, since this has stopped, there has been a gradual decrease in parents and carers being involved in nurseries because of the time and training needed. Managers are increasingly under more pressure to access more funds so that they are not dependent on education departments and, at the same time, to keep fees low. Because of the above reasons, I do feel that in the near future we will see a decrease in community-run nurseries and the increase in privately-run day nurseries which is not what I want.

Marcia Myers, Childcare Manager, Birmingham Settlement Community Nursery

I had been working for various childcare establishments with Birmingham City Council for six years. I had gained a wide range of valuable experience working with children and families. I remember browsing through the *Evening Mail*, a large advert caught my attention about a community nursery opening in Ladywood. The phrase, 'Run by the community for the community' really caught my eye. I found myself ringing up for an application form; one mouth later I was being interviewed for the position of deputy nursery manager. A management committee member who was an active member of the local community showed me around the nursery, which was part of a school that had been closed down. The refurbishments were nearly complete. As the committee member showed me around she took pleasure in telling me how long it had taken to get off the ground. Now finally the dream was becoming a reality. Her enthusiasm and excitement really made me want the position even more. I … soon began working with the manager to recruit a team of seven workers. One of the aims of the nursery was to employ at least half of the staff from the community. This was my first experience of shortlisting and interviewing. This seemed really daunting. After interviewing over 20 applicants we employed a team of seven qualified and unqualified workers. A lot of hard work went into getting the nursery open – the staff and management committee all started getting to know each other. Babywood Community Nursery opened in October 1999. The team jelled together and in no time it seemed like we had all been working together for years. The staff built an atmosphere of mutual trust and understanding for the children and parents and each other. The nursery cared for a high percentage of one-parent families. Many single mums when they first arrived at nursery were very timid and lacked confidence. With the support of staff and other parents who they knew from the community all of these parents strived to increase their knowledge and personal skills. It was a joy to see young women being empowered, giving them the confidence to seek well-paid employment. The children benefited from social interaction with adults and their peers, many children's development was enhanced by the stimulating activities and events organised by the staff. My time spent at Babywood was one of the best experiences I have had. It was wonderful to be able to support staff, children and parents. We were all one big family …

During my time at Babywood I became involved in Small Steps. In 1990, an informal support initiative was set up for community nurseries of charitable or non-profit making status in specific areas of the city. The aim of these nurseries was to provide the maximum number of places at the lowest possible cost to residents from the immediate locality. Small Steps is a fully constituted funded body. Today the network is made up of 15 nurseries from across the city of Birmingham with valuable input from the Childcare Information Bureau, Birmingham City Councils Economic Development Department, Co-enterprise and the Early Years Development and Childcare Partnership. By bringing nurseries together in the community nursery network, common issues can be worked through and strengths maximised. In addition, sharing information and training needs helps each nursery fulfil its own potential. Small Steps lobbies and participates in consultation regarding childcare issues ... Being a member of Small Steps has been extremely beneficial to myself, ranging from support and advice from mangers within the network to training opportunities which have been available to staff. I am now the Chair of Small Steps and look forward to the network's participation in the ever-changing field of childcare.

I began working at Birmingham Settlement in 1993, which is a large voluntary organisation established in 1899. There has always been some form of work with children at the Settlement. The first nursery school established under the Education Act 1918 encouraged mothers to meet and share experiences with each other. Due to high demand the nursery expanded its provision to 90 places. In addition to its educational work, the nursery also prompted an increase in the children's health through the provision of milk and dinners. The project relocated to new premises in Brearley Street in 1939, it was replaced temporarily by a public health department nursery and by a parents' group which met to discuss the bringing up of children.

Birmingham Settlement Community Nursery opened in 1994. Our aim is to provide quality, affordable childcare primarily to parents in Newtown to take up employment and training opportunities, and to work in conjunction with local employers and relevant agencies to further benefit the community. As a multidisciplinary organisation, the Settlement is able to provide parents with access to a range of services in addition to their childcare. Children's Services is closely linked to the Women's Training Programme, promoting training and employment opportunities and linking crèche facilities directly to the Employment Resource Centre and to places on the in-house training courses run in the same building. In order to keep fees at a level that is affordable to parents, the organisation has made an ongoing commitment to raise additional funds, over and above fees and grant income, to bring down the cost of each place. Since the nursery opened, many children and parents have benefited from the care, support and education provided by a dedicated team of childcare workers. Here is a quote from a letter given to me by a parent:

Words cannot express what the nursery as done for Sally, and how grateful I am for what you and your staff have helped Sally to achieve in the three years that she as been at the Settlement. I praise the nursery for always supporting me and other parents. I will feel like a part of my family is missing when we leave.

For me working in community nurseries is not just about caring for children but caring for the whole family.

Notes

Acknowledgements

1. The actual names of the people involved in community nurseries are used in acknowledging them, however, for the sake of anonymity, the names of parents and children are not.
2. This group was set up specifically for the purpose of this community nurseries study.
3. The various research projects that were carried out in this book are mentioned in note 1 relating to Chapter 2, note 15 relating to Chapter 6 and a study of the success of Marcus Garvey which is discussed in Chapter 5.

Chapter 1

1. Randell, V and Fisher, K (2001) Child daycare provision: explaining local variations. *Children and Society* 15, 3, pp. 170-80
2. Penn, H (1997) *Comparing Nurseries: The experiences of children and staff in Day Nurseries in Spain, Italy and the UK*. Paul Chapman
3. Early Years National Training Organisation, National Day Nurseries Association, Department for Education and Employment, Improvement and Development Agency (1999) *Independent Day Nursery Workforce Survey 1998, England*
4. Cohen, B and Fraser, N (1990) *Childcare in a Modern Welfare System: Towards a new national policy*, Institute for Public Policy Research
5. Osgood, J and Sharp, C (2000) *Developing Early Education and Childcare Services for the 21st Century*. National Foundation for Education Research
6. McQuail, S and Pugh, G (1995) *The Effective Organisation of Early Childhood Services*. National Children's Bureau

Chapter 2

1. Moss, P and Penn, H (1996) *Transforming Nursery Education.* Paul Chapman

2. OECD (2000) *OECD Country Note: Early Childhood and Care Policy in the United Kingdom.* DfEE

3. DfEE (2001) *A Nursery in Every Neighbourhood.* DfEE

4. Holterman, S (2001) *Children's Centres: Exploring the costs and delivery of a national scheme.* Daycare Trust

5. Hood, S (2001) *The State of London's Children.* Office for London Children's Rights Commissioner

6. Putnam, R (2001) *Bowling Alone.* Simon and Schuster

7. The London Nursery Campaign, forerunner of the Daycare Trust, published in 1980 a guide to setting up community nurseries called *The Do-It-Yourself Nursery.* This gives a summary of the kind of ideas which informed the community nursery movement.

8. Tizard, B (1986) *The Care of Young Children.* Thomas Coram Research Unit

9. Duncan, S and Edwards, R eds. (1997) *Single Mothers in an International Context: Mothers or workers?* UCL Press

10. See note 9 above

11. Children's Community Centre (1974) *Our Experiences of Collective Childcare.* 123 Dartmouth Park Hill

12. Abbott, L and Nutbrown, C eds. (2001) *Experiencing Reggio Emilia: Implications for pre-school provision.* The Open University Press

13. Saraceno, C (1977) *Experiencia y Teoria de las Comunas Infantiles.* Fontanella

14. Penn, H (1997) *Comparing Nurseries.* Paul Chapman

15. Grover, C (1999) *Childcare in the Community: Community Nurseries in England.* Daycare Trust

16. House of Commons (2001) *Education and Employment Committee: Early years follow up.* The Stationery Office. (pp.5–7) Evidence from the manager of Handsworth Community Nursery

17. *Nursery World*, July 2001

18. Penn, H and Gough, D (2001) The price of a loaf of bread: conceptions of family support. *Children & Society* 15. forthcoming.

19. Clarke, A and Moss, P (2001): *Listening to Young Children.* National Children's Bureau

20. OECD (2001) *Starting strong: Thematic Review of Early Education and Care in Twelve Countries.* OECD. Paris

21. See note 20 above

22. See note 20 above

Chapter 3

1. The majority of the data on which this chapter is based was collected for the Daycare Trust. A fuller version of the results appears in Grover, C 1999, *Childcare in the Community: Community nurseries in England*, Daycare Trust (info@daycaretrust.org.uk). The research was funded by the Department of Health and Bridge House Estates.

2. For the sake of anonymity the names of the nurseries have been changed, as have the names of the respondents and their children.

3. Tony Blair, writing in the *Daily Mail*, 10 February 1999.

4. Hansard (1998) Welfare reform, 28 October 1998, issue no. 1800, cols. 339–355. Comments of Alistair Darling, Secretary of State for Social Security

5. Labour Party (2001) *Ambitions for Britain*. Labour Party

6. Harman, H (1997) A Hand up, not a hand out. *Fabian Review*, 109, 1, 4–5.

7. Brown, G (1999) Chancellor's Speech to the Newspaper Conference, 22 July 1999 *Treasury New Release*. www.hm-treasury.gov.uk/speech/cx21799.html

8. Department for Education and Employment, Department of Social Security and Ministers for Women (1998) *Meeting the Childcare Challenge: A framework and consultation document*. The Stationery Office

9. Social Security Committee (1998) *The Case for Social Security Reform*, Minutes of Evidence, given by Harriet Harman Wednesday 25 February 1998 HC587–1. The Stationery Office

10. Grover, C and Stewart, J (2000) Modernising welfare: New Labour and social security, *Social Policy and Administration*, 33, 3, 235–252

11. Grover, C and Stewart, J (forthcoming 2002) *The Work Connection: The role of social security in regulating social and economic life in Britain*. Palgrave

12. Holterman, S (2001) *Children's Centres: Exploring the costs and delivery of a national scheme*. Daycare Trust

13. Department for Education and Employment (2000) New places for 1.6 million children by 2004 in childcare expansion, *Press Notice 2000/045*. DfEE

14. Jones, C and Novak, T (1999) *Poverty, Welfare and the Disciplinary State*, Routledge, Quotation cited from Haughey, 1998

15. Ginsburg, N (1979) *Class, Capital and Social Policy*. Macmillan

16. Grover, C and Stewart, J (forthcoming 2002) *The Work Connection: the role of social security in regulating social and economic life in Britain*. Palgrave

17. Shaw, A and others (1996) *Moving Off Income Support. Barriers and Bridges*. HMSO

18. Daycare Trust (1997) *The Childcare Gap*. Briefing Paper 1. Daycare Trust

19. Daycare Trust (2001) 'Parents pick up the tab as childcare costs spiral close to £6000 a year for just one two year old'. *News from Daycare Trust*, 5 February. Daycare Trust

20. Vernon, J and Smith, C (1994) *Day Nurseries at the Crossroads: Meeting the challenge of child care in the nineties*. National Children's Bureau

21. Davis, M (1990) *City of Quartz: Excavating the Future of Los Angeles*. Verso

22. See note 21 above

23. The survey did, however, discover a small number of community nurseries that are exclusively for children from specific minority ethnic and religious groups

Chapter 4

1. This is a very modest account of what amounts to a Samaritan's service. One of the author's has a child who attended Ackroyd and so has first hand knowledge of the many ways in which local families have been supported and helped.

Chapter 5

1. DfES (2001) *Building Neighbourhood Nurseries*. DfES

Chapter 6

1. Marcus Garvey is regarded as a national hero of Jamaica for his contribution in the 1920s and 1930s in attempting to unite black people primarily in the USA, Jamaica and, to a lesser extent, Britain, and to instil in them a pride in their race.

2. Black here refers to people of African-Caribbean descent

3. Apart from using the actual names of the nursery and the first head, who agreed that we may do so, for the sake of anonymity the identities of other participants, has been changed

4. Clark, D (1987) The concept of community education, in Allen, G, Bastiani, J, Martin, I and Richards, K Eds *Community Education: An agenda for educational reform*. Open University Press

5. Fletcher, C The meaning of 'community' in community education, *in* Allen, G, Bastiani, J, Martin, I and Richards, K *eds.* (1987) *Community Education: An agenda for educational reform*. Open University Press

6. The study was carried out at Nottingham Trent University and funded by fast-track Research Assessment Exercise (RAE) finance

7. Rich, P (1994) *Prospero's Return?: Historical essays on race and culture and British society*. Hansib Publications

8. Community Relations Commission (1975) *Wednesday's Children: A report on under-fives provision in Handsworth*. Lozells Social Development Centre

9. McCalla, D (2001) The academic and the community meet: Two, black female voices, *International Journal of Inclusive Education*, 5 4, 1–19

10. Coard, B (1971) *How the West Indian Child is Made Educationally Sub-normal in the British School System.* New Beacon

11. Gillborn, D (1997) Young, black and failed by school: the market, education reform and black students. *International Journal of Inclusive Education*, 1, 65–87

12. Blair, M, Bourne, and others (1998) *Making the Difference: Teaching and learning strategies in successful multi-ethnic schools.* DfEE

13. Morgan, S (1986) Practice in a community nursery for black children, in Shama, A, Cheetham, J and Small, J *eds. Social Work with Black Children and their Families.* Batsford, 69–70

14. Grover, C (1999) *Childcare in the Community: Community nurseries in England.* Daycare Trust

15. Penn, H (2000) Policy and practice in childcare and nursery education, *Journal of Social Policy*, 29: 1, 37–55

16. Cutler, T and Waine, B (1994) *Managing the Welfare State: The politics of public sector management.* BERG

17. Powell, M (2000) (Ed.) *New Labour, New Welfare State? The 'Third Way' in British social policy.* Policy Press

18. Annancy stories are fictional Caribbean stories of a spider. The stories demonstrate a moral or social meaning

19. Marcus Garvey Nursery holds an annual graduation ceremony for children leaving the nursery in that academic year

20. See note 8 above

21. Feinberg W (1998) *Common Schools/Uncommon Identities: National unity and cultural difference.* Yale University Press

22. Graham, J and Bowling, B (1995) *Young People and Crime.* HMSO

23. Gillborn, D and Gipps, C (1996) *Recent Research on the Achievement of Ethnic Minority Pupils.* HMSO

24. Parsons, C and others (1996) *Exclusion from School: The public cost.* Commission for Racial Equality

25. See note 11 above

26. Pearce, N and Hillman, J (1998) *Wasted Youth: Raising achievement and tackling school exclusion.* Institute for Public Policy Research

27. Social Exclusion Union (1998). *Truancy and School Exclusions.* HMSO.

28. Ball, C. (1994) *Start Right: The importance of early learning.* Royal Society of Arts.

29. David T, Curtis, A, Siraj-Batchford, I (1992) *Effective Teaching in the Early Years: Fostering children's learning in nurseries and in infant classes.* OMEP.

30. 'Nuff' here translates as 'a lot of'

Chapter 7

1. Penn, H and Lloyd, E (2001) *The Role of Nursery Schools and the Voluntary Sector.* Forthcoming. A version of this is available on *www.ucl.ac.uk/education*

2. Daycare Trust, reported in *the Guardian*, 4 July 2001

3. Penn, H and Gough, D (2001) The Price of a Loaf of Bread: Some Conceptions of Family Support. *Children & Society,* 15. forthcoming.

4. See report on nursery chains in *Nursery World,* July 2001

5. Cabinet Office (2000) *Reaching Out: The role of central and local government.* Performance and Innovation Unit, Cabinet Office

6. OECD (2001) *Starting Strong: Thematic Review of Early Education and Care in Twelve Countries.* OECD

7. Penn, H (2001) Maintains a Good Pace to Lessons: Inconsistencies and contextual factors affecting Ofsted Inspections of Nursery Schools, *British Educational Research Journal,* forthcoming. A version of this is available on *www.uel.ac.uk/education*

8. See note 7 above

9. See note 7 above

10. Department of Social Security (1998) *A New Contract for Welfare: Principles into practice,* The Stationery Office

11. Pascal, C, Bertram T, Gasper, M, Mould, C, Ramsden, F and Saunders, M (2001) *Research to Inform the Evaluation of Early Excellence Centres Pilot Programme.* DfEE Research Report 259

12. See note 11 above

13. Moss, P and others (2000) *A Review of Childminding.* Thomas Coram Research Unit. Research Report.

14. DfEE (2001) *A Nursery in Your Neighbourhood.* DfEE Publications

15. The comments about EYDCPs are drawn from research on EYDCPs undertaken by Penn, H, Raynes, N and McLaughlin, H for the Children's Society. At the time of writing this is an internal report for the Children's Society, but it is anticipated that the material will be published in 2002.

16. Eisenstadt, N (2001) *The Sure Start Programme.* Paper given at DfEE/OECD conference, Lancaster House, April 2001

17. Moss, P and Penn, H (1996) *Transforming Nursery Education.* Paul Chapman.

18. European Union Childcare Network (1999) *Quality Targets for Early Childhood Services.* Brussels. DG5

19. See note 11 above

20. McCalla, D and Griffiths, M (2001) Social justice in education: the politics of presence, *School Field.* Impress

21. Holterman, S (2001) *Children's Centres: Exploring the costs and delivery of a national scheme*. Daycare Trust

22. See note 21 above

Appendix 2

1.   The participants have consented for us to use their actual names and the actual names of the nurseries concerned. However, the names of the children have been changed for anonymity

2.   Whalley, M (1997) *Working with Parents*. Hodder and Stoughton

3.   Wigfall, V and Moss, P (2001) *More than the Sum of its Parts? A study of a multi-agency childcare network*. National Children's Bureau

4.   Clark, A and Moss, P (2001) *Listening to Young Children*. National Children's Bureau

Index

123 Community Nursery 9-12

Ackroyd community nursery 12-14
    case study 35-9
adult literacy 72
African-Caribbean children 52-6
Austin Road Day Nursery 84

Babywood 85-6
benefits 67
Big Wheel nursery 23, 24
Birmingham Settlement Community
    Nursery 86-7
black community see Marcus
    Garvey EYC
Bowlby, John 9

Caribbean children 52-6
Castle nursery 30
    on private care 31-2
Centres of Early Excellence 69-70
childcare
    continuity 5-6
    cost of 24-6
    early education divide 7
Childcare Tax Credit 25, 28
childminders 70-1
communities and nursery provision 7-8
community nurseries 8-12, 77
    aims 11-12
    and daycare 29-32
    defined by researchers 17-18

interviews and questionnaires 19
overseas 14
professionalism 10
Sure Start 69
continuity of care 5-6
cost
    childcare 24-6
    private daycare 30-32

daycare provision 29-32
discrimination 48-9, 50

Early Years Development and Care
    Partnerships see EYDCPs
education
    for parents 59
    provision 6
employment
    enabling 58-9
    and nursery provision 21
EYDCPs 72-5

fees 65-6
    Ackroyd 37
Foundations Day Nursery 81-2
funding
    Ackroyd 38
    community nurseries 11, 13
    constraints, Marcus Garvey 50
    from government 67-8
    nursery education 6, 26-8

government
    funding from 67-8
    policy 1
grant, Ackroyd 35, 36, 38

High Peaks nursery 22-3, 24
    on serving the community 30
Holterman, Sally 77

interviews 19
    Marcus Garvey 55-6

lone mothers 22

Marcus Garvey EYC 14, 15
    case study 47-64
    origins 48-50
    parents' involvement 57-60
    research conducted 47-8
    and the wider community 60-2
mothers, involving 23
Myers, Marcia 85-7

National Childcare Campaign 11
National Childcare Strategy 15, 19,
    20, 66-7, 71
neighbourhood nurseries 7, 20, 41,
    71-2, 77
New Opportunities Fund 20
nurseries in the survey 79-80
nursery provision 67-8
    available today 5
    cohesion, lack of 68, 77
    criteria 76-7
    free places 28
    maintaining numbers attending 29
    private 30-32
    and schools 68
    types of 5, 6-7
    workshop on 1

OECD report 7, 15
Organisation for Economic
    Cooperation and Development
    see OECD report

parents
    education for 59
    experiences of 81-4
    help for 24
    Marcus Garvey 57-60
Patrick, Caroline 84
Plowden Report 9
private daycare, cost 30-31
professionalism and the community
    nursery 10

Reggio Emilia nurseries 12
Robert Owen Early Years Centre 14,
    case study 41-6
    funding 43
    origins 8-12

self esteem, lone mothers 22-4
single parents see lone mothers
Small Steps nursery 85-6
social
    exclusion 7-8, 20, 21-6, 56
    relationships 11
    services 74-5
staff experiences 84-7
Sure Start 69, 74

training for parents 24
Tree House nursery, funding 28

UN Declaration on the Rights of the child 14

volunteers 10

Walsall Council 82-4
welfare system reforms 19
working mothers 9
workshop, nursery provision 1